ABOUT CANADA
MEDIA

Peter Steven

About Canada Series

Fernwood Publishing • Halifax & Winnipeg

To the memory of Yvan Patry (1948-1999), Québécois filmmaker

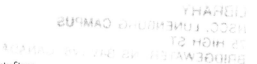

Editing: Brenda Conroy
Cover design: John van der Woude
Printed and bound in Canada by Hignell Book Printing

Published in Canada by Fernwood Publishing
32 Oceanvista Lane, Black Point, Nova Scotia, B0J 1B0
and 748 Broadway Avenue, Winnipeg, MB R3G 0X3
www.fernwoodpublishing.ca

Fernwood Publishing Company Limited gratefully acknowledges the financial support of the Government of Canada through the Canada Book Fund, the Canada Council for the Arts, the Nova Scotia Department of Tourism and Culture, the Manitoba Department of Culture, Heritage and Tourism under the Manitoba Publishers Marketing Assistance Program and the Province of Manitoba, through the Book Publishing Tax Credit, for our publishing program.

Library and Archives Canada Cataloguing in Publication

Steven, Peter, 1950-
About Canada : media / Peter Steven.

(About Canada)
Includes bibliographical references.
ISBN 978-1-55266-447-6 (pbk.).–ISBN 978-1-55266-459-9 (bound)

1. Mass media–Canada. I. Title. II. Series: About Canada series

P92.C3S74 2011   302.230971   C2011-903271-6

CONTENTS

1. A CRISIS OF QUALITY

On June 23, 2010, Canadians were startled with some big news in the media world. No, Oprah wasn't joining the CBC. But some other ideas from south of the border had washed up in Montreal. A press conference had been called by Quebecor, one of Canada's biggest media corporations. The other media outlets sensed something newsworthy. Kory Teneycke, an aggressive conservative who had previously served as Stephen Harper's communications director, bounded onstage wearing a big, pale blue tie. He was here to reveal the birth of a new television network — Sun TV.

Spectators immediately made the connection with Fox News in the U.S. when Teneycke boasted: "We're taking on the mainstream media. We're taking on smug, condescending, often irrelevant journalism. We're taking on political correctness. We will not be a state broadcaster offering boring news by bureaucrats, for elites and paid for by taxpayers."[1] Now, said the wags, Canada would have a Fox News North, something to challenge that smug, condescending CBC. Starting in 2011, Quebecor's new venture promised to bring us cheap opinion shows in the mould of Fox News, what Nancy Franklin, of the *New Yorker*, calls the screech shows. The gathering of actual news by professional journalists needn't take up much of the budget.

The Canadian media enjoy high ratings at home and abroad

for their serious journalism, their advanced telecommunications and their lively entertainment in radio, film and TV. As my dad reminds me: "Canadian comedians Wayne and Shuster appeared on the *Ed Sullivan Show* more than any other comedians." The National Film Board of Canada has long been admired for its high quality documentaries and animation. CBC Radio draws respect for its drama and documentary work. The *Toronto Star, Le Devoir* and other papers have sent many excellent journalists to work internationally. Canadian actors, writers and directors have achieved international fame. And beginning in the 1970s, Canada acquired a reputation for its satellite and digital communications.

But is that reputation still deserved? Has the decent work produced in the past been maintained? On the contrary, it is clear that our media system has entered a crisis of quality. And Canada's media problems are not unique. The media's crisis of quality plagues other countries as well though it takes different forms. Throughout the book I look at two related questions: What sorts of media do we have? And how do we assess it? While questions about the overall value of Canadian media for both news and entertainment present us with many complex issues, on one point the evidence is clear. What we have now is inferior to what existed ten or twenty years ago.

Funding Cuts

Starting in the 1990s, federal governments, both Conservative and Liberal, began to cut steadily their support to the CBC. This has resulted in damage to news and drama operations, as well as the corporation's reputation. Local newscasts and more expensive dramas have faced annihilation, with documentaries also suffering, especially after 800 jobs got slashed in May 2009. Conservatives particularly loathe the CBC because they perceive a liberal, central Canada bias in both news and serious dramas and because of their general distaste for some types of state support (against the arts, for the tar sands). The Chrétien and Martin Liberals cut the CBC in the 1990s using the excuse of deficit reduction but also because of lobbying from private media giants claiming that the CBC enjoys a competitive advantage. Pressure even came from life-time Liberal Izzy Asper, then head of CanWest Global.

Even critics of the CBC understand how government cuts have drastically affected program quality. Our national broadcaster now relies more and more on advertising and specializes in the cheapest-made programs and U.S. clones, such as *Dragon's Den,* and non-stop, stand-up comedy. These cuts have also affected children's TV, one of Canada's best media achievements. In the past ten years the number of programs has fallen, budgets for programs have dropped 14 percent, and the level of government funding has dropped significantly. A 2009 report states that Canada's reputation as a world leader in children's live action and animation is "at risk."[2]

As for basic telecommunications, which provide the foundation for our entire online world, we face another crisis. While it may seem to young urbanites that "everyone is online," in rural areas, and First Nations communities especially, the digital gap is widening. Access to a computer and modem is no longer sufficient — you must have broadband to keep up. Two international studies from 2009 and 2010, out of Oxford and Harvard universities, make this clear.[3] These studies show that the high price for many customers and the slow speed of delivery are now serious problems in Canada, particularly in rural and sparsely populated areas. The Oxford study believes that "Canada is woefully positioned for future internet usage... because of a lack of investment" by the large telecommunications providers.

Job Losses in the Media

December 2008 — 560 at CanWest; 600 at Quebecor
2008 — 270 at Torstar
2009 — 800 at CBC
June 2010 — 121 at Torstar
September 2010 — 50 at *Edmonton Journal* with more to come at Postmedia

Canada's music recording and distribution systems provide a partial exception to this bleak picture, although racial and ethnic minorities are under-served. Unfortunately, commercial radio, which provides a key outlet for music, has done little to support the full range of Canadian artists and thus fits with the pattern of decline. By law, radio stations must play 35 percent Canadian content but this certainly doesn't guarantee a diverse playlist. Although radio stations now seem proud of the home-grown music they air, it's useful to remember that they vehemently opposed such quotas when they were introduced in the 1970s. They claimed then that Canadians didn't care about home-grown music and that Big Brother, i.e., the State, should not dictate what we hear. Today, the same groups call for more cuts to the CBC for the same reasons. Now, many commercial stations have abandoned music entirely, substituted with cheap forms of talk-radio programming — most hosted by a range of opinionated conservatives, from old-style Tories to pentacostal right-wingers.

Commercial Media

Canada suffers from one of the least competitive news systems in the Western world. An ever smaller group of media giants now controls both news and entertainment. These companies include BCE, Quebecor, Torstar, Rogers, Shaw and the Postmedia chain. This is hardly a new situation and anyone who has studied the Canadian media since the 1970s has agreed — even the Senate expressed concern about media concentration in its 2006 report.[4] What seemed like too few owners in the 1970s now seems like a crowd.

If we broaden the scope beyond the daily news to look at book publishing, the situation gets grimmer all the time, with Chapters and the U.S. giant Amazon in control of at least 80 percent of the retail market. Canadian nationalists who may prefer to get their books from Chapters should know that the money behind its near monopoly, Onex Corporation, has awfully deep pockets and has on and off exercised substantial control of film exhibition as well.

Chapters' CEO, Heather Reisman, is married to Gerry Schwartz, the CEO of Onex.

News and entertainment media that make profits their top priority have most often produced high quality, valuable work when commercial success is measured in the long term. Today, however, corporate media have shifted their focus to short-term profits. This creates major problems because it discourages investment in quality or more innovative programs and initiatives, which may take longer to gain a foothold. The scramble for short-term profits fosters cost cutting in the production of entertainment and news. Canadian broadcasters now refuse to purchase more than a few episodes of a drama or comedy for fear that a program won't draw high audience ratings. This leads to shows being born in a blaze of publicity, only to be doused after a few episodes. Production costs go up, and the writers and actors don't get a fair chance to develop. This system also favours the quick sensation and the easy formula — cop shows galore (*The Border, The Bridge, Flashpoint, The Line, Republic of Doyle, Rookie Blue*).

As for the news, the push for short-term profits among newspapers and broadcasters has led not only to a significant loss of journalists and editors, it has resulted in fewer long-form stories and less emphasis on investigative reporting. In the TV world, cuts have decimated local news programs, replacing them with regional or national digests. For example, as recently as 2002, CBC in Toronto produced a one-hour local news program for 6:00 and 11:00 pm. This included items of serious journalism on social issues, health care and municipal politics — not simply fires, sports and accidents. That local journalism has disappeared. Way back in 1992, Dean Jobb, a veteran journalist, registered his anger about these trends in news when he covered the Westray, Nova Scotia, mine disaster: "There's a real shift in the media these days. It's the trivial now, it's the fluff, it's the feelies, it's the people angles, human interest… is that all there is to this mine disaster?"[5]

Finally, the frenzy for short-term profits has saddled us with bad and weak management. Conrad Black and his one-time pals, notably David Radler, made their mark in the '70s, '80s and '90s, by slashing jobs, manipulating employee pensions and generally degrading newspapers across the country.[6] Predictably, none of the other major media considered this newsworthy until Black's U.K. and U.S. investors blew the whistle and sent him to prison. Most media managers aren't criminals, but often they're bad at business, with eyes bigger than their stomachs. Witness Leonard Asper, former head of CanWest, who purchased Alliance Atlantis, the film and TV giant, in 2007, thus plunging his company $2.3 billion further into debt and aligning itself in a risky venture with Goldman Sachs of New York, an outfit soon to be disgraced in the banking scandals. CanWest never recovered and collapsed in 2009, but Asper continues to spin his tale of woe about tough times due to poor advertising revenues.

What about the Internet?

Those who believe in the power of the internet proclaim that we now have more news and information than ever before. And surely, they say, that makes up for any shortcomings in the mainstream news sources. There may be some truth to this but the situation is considerably more complicated. In Canada, as in most of the world's rich countries, the elites and most academics have access through the internet to more news and information of all kinds. University and college students likewise can, if motivated, take advantage of the incredible range of information online. For the average citizen, however, who hasn't the time, money, access to broadband services or specialized research skills, cruising the internet is not a reality. Most still rely on the dominant media of TV, radio and newspapers, and in all these cases there is less news and public affairs material than twenty years ago. TV news shows are shorter and more celebrity-driven, with scant local content. Newspapers employ fewer reporters and print shorter articles. Commercial radio has sunk to the worst it has ever been in reporting or showcasing Canadian content. CBC

Radio is perhaps the exception to this, reflected in its high citizen support, although a leaked internal survey of reporters in April 2010 revealed great unhappiness about the new trends of combining TV and radio reporting.[7] "The survey paints a picture of a creative team demoralized by decisions that have diminished the quality of its work controlled by managers who do not understand radio. Some low lights of the survey: 81 percent reject the notion (52.4 percent strongly) that the integration of TV and radio has benefited National Radio News programming."

When it comes to accessing information, the class divide is greater than before. I return in later chapters to discuss the internet and what's known as the digital divide. And, as I outline in Chapter Two, the coverage of international news is a catastrophe. Thus, the quantity and quality of material available to most people has diminished. The elites are getting more and everyone else gets less.

Conservative Deep Freeze

Canada's major political parties exhibit few differences when it comes to policies about the media. All accept the status quo of government regulation and private ownership. All value the CBC as a useful, albeit unruly, arm of the state. Nevertheless, since the election of Stephen Harper's government in 2003 some particular problems have emerged. Harper shows a deep distrust of the national media and goes out of his way to limit communication. He also insists on a tightly scripted message for all his party members. This attitude reflects his Western conservative roots, which see the national media as representing elitist easterners and closet socialists. Because Harper's political base distrusts the news media he feels he can ignore reporters and journalists.

Conservative Party supporters also place little stock in subsidies to the arts and Canadian-bred media. They favour a free-market approach in which merit is judged solely by sales and what they call main street popularity. This has encouraged the government to cut

CBC funds further than the Liberals did and to threaten government grants to film and TV producers.

Another major problem with the Harper agenda is its deepening freeze on access to public information. Canadians now face a systematic attempt by the federal government to block access into anything the least embarrassing — on Afghanistan, the tar sands, the war on terror and so on. "Since the tongue-lashing the Harper government received from the advisory panel on Afghanistan," says journalist David McKay, "little evidence of increased openness has appeared. The difficulty in determining the war's cost provides a good example."[8] Since none of the other parties differ substantially on these vital issues there's little political support for journalists digging for that information. Even Canada's Information Commissioner has stated that our access to information risks being "totally obliterated."[9]

The deep freeze extends to attitudes about climate change. Internal documents leaked from Environment Canada in 2010 revealed that "scientists have noticed a major reduction in the number of requests" for information "particularly from high-profile media." The report concluded: "Media coverage of climate change science, our most high-profile issue, has been reduced by over 80 percent." This followed new rules set out by the federal government in 2007 "which required senior federal scientists to seek permission from the government prior to giving interviews," said reporter Mike De Souza. "In many cases, the policy also required them to get approval from supervisors of written responses to the questions submitted by journalists before any interview." For example, said De Souza, this occurred during "an investigation into the government's views and policies on global-warming science that was conducted by Climate Action Network Canada, a coalition of environmental groups."[10]

The Big Challenges

Although Canada is not alone in this crisis of quality of the media, we do face special problems by living in the shadow of the U.S.

The reality is that the Canadian media primarily send out U.S. not Canadian content — our media "is a conduit for the distribution of non-Canadian cultural goods."[11] Like ostriches we continue to repeat that we can relax — at least we're better than the Americans. Our small size and frequent inwardness have not made us of much interest to outsiders. Conversely, engaged citizens in the U.S., Britain and France have insisted that their media be part of the political debate; because media wield power, they need to be monitored. Few of us feel that compulsion with Canadian media.

Our media lack a critical backbone. They seem incapable of playing a real watchdog role, independent of the state and the large corporations. Even the *Toronto Star*, which fashions itself as a liberal standard-bearer, has cut back its investigative reporting in recent years. The same with CBC Radio and TV. The *Star* and the CBC employ some of the most capable journalists anywhere, people like Jim Coyle and Carol Off, but these reporters seldom get the opportunity to undertake significant investigative work. Or they're being pushed aside by penny-ante distractions like cocaine-snorting ex-MPs.

We might hope that the entry into Canada, in May 2010, of Al-Jazeera, the international, Arab-based broadcaster, will lead to a shakeup at least for international news, because our major media have slashed their international coverage (as is the case everywhere in the West). The old media is in crisis, but it is not due to their business models. They will survive, but they're not the media we need. It's a crisis of quality.

Journalists as Subjects

Aside from the police, the most difficult subjects are journalists.... They're particularly aware of what it means to have something about them published in a magazine or a newspaper because they do it all the time. —David Hayes, former media columnist at *Toronto Life*, quoted in "In Your Face," by Marco Ursi, *Ryerson Journalism Review*, Spring 2006.

2. FORMS, STYLES AND GENRES

Realism is the key word regarding forms, styles and genres that have been central in Canadian media. Since the 1950s, followers of Canadian entertainment have described our films, TV and radio as low-key, natural and gritty. This view made sense in the past because of the high profile of the documentary films of the National Film Board, which had gained international attention. Films shot on location, without elaborate studio sets and huge budgets, lent themselves to realism as well. For a people largely invisible onscreen and unheard on the radio, seeing and hearing Canadians was a treat — just what was needed as a first step for a young media culture.

This followed an international trend made famous in postwar Italy, where the thirst for a new cinema to accompany a new society took the name neo-realism. Neo-realism as a film movement was more than a style or set of subjects; it explicitly rejected what had gone before, especially what prevailed in Hollywood. Indian cinema after independence produced realist films as well, such as Satyajit Ray's great *Apu* trilogy (1955–59). Even the well-established British cinema took up "kitchen sink" realism in the late 1950s, as did Hollywood itself with its social problem pictures. Although Canadian cinema was never as focused or conscious, it nevertheless took realism as a useful term to suggest difference from the mainstream.

When critics wish to celebrate how Canadian films are different from those put out by Hollywood, they often gravitate to films far from the standard stylized genres, such as musicals, westerns and crazy comedies. Canadian films, with minimal stories, a mix of humour and drama, actual locations and obviously small budgets, seemed so much more "realistic" than Hollywood fare. For Quebec film and television in particular, the concept of realism held sway. Quebec's drama series, or *téléroman*, presented a strikingly different culture in terms of language, history, religion and economics. In addition, the internationally influential documentary movements that captured attention in the late 1950s emerged not by filming from a distance but from among working-class people — what the pioneering cinematographer and director Michel Brault refers to as "wide-angle cinema."

In recent years, however, many historians and viewers have realized that realism was only one style in a much broader palette. By emphasizing realism, we have ignored other forms and genres and have not paid enough attention to what producers and directors have created. For example, radio drama and innovative radio reporting stretch back to the 1930s in Canada. These often used expressive, even experimental elements rather than realism to develop characters, set a mood, suggest a location or present ideas. And many of these radio characteristics were pulled into TV and films as the 1950s moved on. As well, although realism as a general style has characterized much film and TV, writers, directors and actors have often relied on a few standard character types — the lovable loser, the outsider, the kook.

The Canadian fantastic and gothic have been present nearly from the beginning, says the film theorist Jim Leach. In his study of English Canadian and Québécois fiction and documentary, he shows how films described as realist often contain other elements meant to disturb viewers or complicate stories and characters. The horror films of David Cronenberg are an obvious example, but Leach argues that such elements turn up in many other films. For example,

Paul Almond's trilogy made with his wife, Genevieve Bujold, *Isabel, Act of the Heart* and *Journey* (1968, 1970, 1972), "were too dark and disturbing to qualify" as part of the realist tradition, but neither did they fit within "mainstream commercial cinema."[1] Leach places these within the genre of the fantastic, which "depends on the 'hesitation' experienced by a person who knows only the laws of nature, confronting an apparently supernatural event."[2] As for the gothic, the historical dramas *Kamouraska* (Claude Jutra, 1973) and *The Far Shore* (Joyce Wieland, 1976) focus on the subjective experience of women trapped in traditional marriages. One reviewer called Jutra's film *Wuthering Heights* on the St. Lawrence.[3]

Non-realist elements also appear in such documentary/fiction hybrids as Michel Brault's *Les Ordres* (1974), inspired by the October 1970 FLQ crisis, and in Allan King's *A Married Couple* (1969). King's film is clearly a realist project with apparently little intervention from the film crew — we seem to be invisible watchers, relentlessly following a couple in their home who fight their way to a marriage breakup. But the film is so intense and the characters so uninhibited by the camera that their actions become a dramatic performance. The film "hovers between claims to documentary authenticity and fictional artifice.... King insisted that 'what was going on isn't really acting,' but he recognized that 'they were making things up... and therefore it's not real.'"[4]

"Gentle comedy is our forte," says *Globe and Mail* television critic John Doyle of Canadian-made TV. He argues that "we see ourselves as a gentle people, proud of being peace-makers, not war-mongers." For example, "*Little Mosque on the Prairie* (2006–) made the American media curious because it has a comic premise that's outrageous in the context of mainstream U.S. network TV. The idea was avant-garde. But in a nutshell," says Doyle "that is the strength of Canadian television — the best of it, by instinct or design, rejects the common ingredients for comedy or drama on American TV and cooks up a distinctly indigenous television culture."[5]

Little Mosque follows in the tradition of CTV's *Corner Gas* (2004–

The Media: A Modern Concept

The contemporary word media still carries a trace of its original Latin meaning of "medium" or "middle." The singular noun, medium, is a link or intermediate agent between places or things; thus, a medium in chemistry holds particles together, or it can be a device of transport for reaching another place. A dog-sled is a medium of transport. So, in the eighteenth century, newspapers began to be called a medium for ideas and advertising. Collectively they became news media. By the twentieth century, with the coming of radio and television and the large companies or government departments that manage them, the new plural sense of the word began to be used.

We now refer to "the media" as entities unto themselves (or even one homogenous thing). The media no longer act simply as devices or neutral carriers of ideas but rather as the source of ideas and meanings. They are a central element of power, with structures, rules and conventions unto themselves. It's in this sense that Marshall McLuhan's phrase "The medium is the message" rings true.

Today, the media include newspapers, cinema, radio and recording, television, the internet and handheld devices. Throughout this book I refer to specific examples, but it is useful to think of the following characteristics that all media hold in common:

- producers and distributors of news, entertainment and information;
- engaged in handling sophisticated technology for recording, distribution and reception;
- distributed to large and socially diverse audiences whose individual members are usually unknown to each other — i.e., "mass" media;
- institutions — not simple companies or government agencies but complex organizations with symbolic functions;
- theoretically accessible to all (there is nothing in the science or technology itself that is designed for some specific group in society — they function primarily as *broad*casters); and
- powerful forces of capitalism in most societies — in economic terms they are hugely wealthy and wield political as well as cultural and ideological power.

What Canada Does Right

Canada's media system has nurtured world-renowned artists, journalists, film directors, writers, actors, radio producers, reporters, war correspondents, muckrakers and wild iconoclasts. In the past, these people often fled for greener pastures in Britain, France and the U.S., but today many see the advantages of Canada as a home base.

Canada has also created a media system that mixes public and private organizations. It balances commercial companies and government regulations, which ensures some degree of universal and affordable access to media. Ottawa at one time also made great efforts to service rural and northern areas through satellite technology. Although the CBC most often operates as an arm of the state rather than a truly *public* broadcaster, it provides considerable space to dissenting views and a range of cultural expressions. The CBC is not a monolithic entity — it is a battleground for conflicting ideas, and it employs people with quite different views of society than its managers.

Canadians find fault with many aspects of the CBC, especially its TV operations, but few would opt for the totally commercial U.S. model (a striking parallel with views on our health-care system). Most Canadians compare the CBC favourably to the U.S. networks in its relation to the government in power. We cringe, for example, at the servile role of the U.S. media in covering their country's never-ending wars and aggressive foreign policy.

In fact, Canadian consumers of media often get the best of both worlds since we can pull in the top U.S. entertainment combined with our much better news system. In one evening I can (without cable or satellite) watch *The Simpsons, Mad Men,* the Leafs lose to the Habs, a superb arts documentary and *The National.* While, this leaves much to be desired, comparatively, such choice ranks high in the world of media.

Canada's political development has also made space for a unique media system in Quebec, which, to some degree, reflects the heritage and global situation of its citizens. Quebec media producers and artists have since the 1960s benefited from higher rates of subsidy, and its media culture is richer because of it.

2009), the CBC's *Degrassi* franchise and the independent *Red Green* (1991–2006). Then there's *Trailer Park Boys* (2001–2007). This might not strike everyone as gentle but it's about as different from U.S. TV as a show can get, with plots that revel in small-time criminal schemes, casual and constant drug use, homosexuality and extreme profanity. Ryan Diduck, a filmmaker and scholar quoted by Doyle, believes that the show reflects Canada's legalization of same-sex marriage and relaxed marijuana laws. For Doyle, it's just a "weird and wonderful.... anti-bourgeois soap opera... a cheerful and loving celebration of life at the bottom."

The U.S. Media

Some argue that our inability to escape the shadow of the U.S. has determined both media institutions and genres. Fully 80 percent of what's shown by Canada's commercial broadcasters is U.S. programming. Many Canadians live solely in a U.S. media world of Hollywood plus the news and entertainment of U.S. TV. Like every other country in the world, except perhaps India, Canadian media always to some degree work in counterpoint to the U.S. They either copy, attack or strive for "something different." And whether producers want it or not, their work inevitably gets compared. One common denominator for all Canadian media is that their production and marketing resources fall well below the U.S. norm. For some Canadians, this creates embarrassment and a feeling of inferiority; for others it shows that we need to emphasize creativity and quality rather than spectacle and glitz. There's a good reason why we don't produce much science fiction.

A new trend — the fashion for dramatic action, lots of gunplay and heroic cops — however, takes us much closer to the U.S. The older tradition of police shows, such as *R.C.M.P.* (1960–61), *Night Heat* (1985–1991) and *Due South* (1994–99) made do with small budgets and low levels of testosterone. The new shows reflect a highly skilled TV and film workforce but an increasingly timid broadcast management that believes we must play the U.S. game. The social-democratic politics of *DaVinci's Inquest* (1998–2005) has been replaced by a fetish for terrorists. The plodders with a conscience have been pushed aside by cool and glamourous SWAT teams. It's too soon to chart a relationship between this kind of show and the rise of right-wing federal politics, but they have developed in tandem. *Flashpoint* (2008–), *The Bridge* (2010), *The Border* (2008–2010) and *Rookie Blue* (2010–) have all become hits in the U.S. In the height of irony, however, *Boston Globe* writer Alex Beam laments these shows' generic American-ness. *Flashpoint*, he says, "celebrates everything the Canadians say they hate about us Americans: It's gratuitously violent and stupid, with the Kevlar-vested lads in blue armed to the teeth with the latest weaponry."[6]

Aboriginal Storytelling

The representation of First Nations peoples in Canadian film, television and radio covers immense ground, with more material than in any other country. Most of this has been made by outsiders, but a strong tradition of Aboriginal work also exists, and the range of styles and politics grows wider all the time.

The first major films on First Nations peoples were immensely complex works of art, yet deeply flawed in their methods. Edward Curtis's *In the Land of the Headhunters* (1914) and Robert Flaherty's *Nanook of the North* (1922) proved to be indispensable records of West Coast and Arctic life in the early twentieth century. Both films were created by white men with significant collaboration from the Aboriginal communities who were portrayed — participants who were eager to have their stories told. Still, Curtis and Flaherty remained firmly in control of their projects and went on to profit considerably. The filmmakers' romantic and stereotyped ideas hurt both films, but most viewers then and now seem to come away with increased awe and respect for the Native people who are depicted. We see dignified people who carry with them complex skills and traditions, along with beautiful but realistically harsh landscapes.

Most films from the 1920s to the 1980s were far worse, saddled by carelessness, exoticism and racism. Fortunately, the NFB in particular supported First Nations filmmakers and produced some remarkable works of art. Its record is much more advanced than those of the CBC, commercial broadcasters and most Canadian museums and art galleries. Many of the NFB films broke ground in formal terms as well, wrenching free from the stodgy essay style. Willie Dunn's fast, angry and experimental *Ballad of Crowfoot* (1968) and the powerful *cinéma vérité* style used in *You Are on Indian Land* (1969), directed by Mort Ransen and Mike Mitchell, still pack a wallop. From Edmonton, the long careers of Gil Cardinal (*Indian Summer: The Oka Crisis*, 2006) and Loretta Todd (*Kainayssini Imanistaisiwa: The People Go On,* 2003) exemplify committed film and TV. "Todd's combination of narrative rigour and stylistic experimentation helped expand perceptions of what an aboriginal film should look or feel like."[7]

The outstanding works of Alanis Obomsawin and Zacharius Kunuk show also what is possible with creative drive, a clear political stance and institutional support. Obomsawin's *Kanehsatake: 270 Years of Resistance* (1993) took her to the centre of the Akwesasne (Oka, Quebec) conflicts in 1990, where she filmed as a committed participant. There is no phony objectivity to this journalism. Kunuk also makes clear where he is positioned. In *Atanarjuat: The Fast Runner* (2001), he works as a contemporary Inuit man struggling to represent the recent past of his ancestors. To do this he created a drama-documentary hybrid, not totally different from Flaherty's form but shaped from a radically different viewpoint. It takes nothing away from these filmmakers to suggest that the formative support from the NFB and the Inuit Broadcasting Corporation (IBC) has helped to strengthen their work.

The 1990s saw Aboriginal film and television gain institutional status, making it possible to create ongoing programs and to sponsor longer range projects. The IBC went on air in 1982, after a long struggle. Its success was a great relief to Inuit elders because the CBC had been trying for years to beam its signal of Canadian and U.S. shows into northern communities. That prospect had spurred Inuit leaders to take the initiative and develop their own programming and distribution system. "The IBC does not produce the regular fare of TV sitcoms and talk shows," states its website. "Instead, IBC producers make programming about one of the richest and enduring cultures in our nation, the Inuit of Canada, in the language Inuit speak... Inuktitut. We produce shows about our kids, our musicians, our politicians, our humour, our issues, etc. No one else can make these shows for us!"

An early success and popular hit was *Super Shamou,* by Peter Tapatai and Barney Pattunguyak, in 1987. Another in the gentle comedy genre, it's corny and goofy, slow-paced, somewhat didactic and very funny. It could have been made nowhere else but the IBC. "*Super Shamou* is a household name," said Pattunguyak. "One time I heard older ladies talking after one of the first shows aired. They were talking about whether he was really flying or not," he said laughing in an interview with Kathleen Lippa. The production has had its share of critics; it was once dubbed "the worst movie in the world.... The flying sequence wasn't great, but that doesn't bother me," says Tapatai.[8]

The Aboriginal People's Television Network, launched in 1999, is viewed throughout the North and carried on standard cable in the South. The schedule during 2010 included the nightly *National News*, which featured the three-part series *Ignored to Death,* on how the health care system treats Aboriginal Peoples. Segments were shot in a number of cities, towns and remote reserves. Also running are a wide range of shows, including the ongoing documentary series *Stories of the Land* and the *Creative Native* and the *Fish Out of Water* comedy series.

Documentary

Documentary has been a central media form in Canada since the Second World War, and within that broad category strong genres have emerged over time. Three conscious movements dominate this history.

The Essay

As with all emerging cinemas, Canada's first significant films were documentaries showing distinct national traits and people never before seen onscreen. At its birth in 1939, the National Film Board took up the authoritative essay-style, then dominant in Britain and the U.S., featuring the booming narration of Lorne Greene. That style of documentary became the norm, and although the NFB later experimented with different forms and new technology, the essay with narration still rules. Most of these films, especially during the war and the 1950s, were distributed non-theatrically, not just in cities but to rural and remote areas, brought by travelling projectionists. Older Canadians will remember the *Canada Carries On* (1940–1959) and *Canada at War* (1962–63) series. John Grierson, the NFB founding director, made expansive claims about the effectiveness of the films and their distribution. Since then some scholars have questioned this effectiveness, but the films strongly affected how Canadians saw the country and each other, which fulfilled the NFB mandate. Later, starting particularly in the 1990s, the NFB produced a much wider range of subjects and documentary styles. The vast majority of these works are liberal or social democratic, feminist, queer positive and relatively diverse in terms of race and ethnicity. Many of the films tackle key social and economic problems in ways that may make governments of the day uncomfortable. Probably the most radical of the NFB staff filmmakers has been Alanis Obomsawin. But overall, the influence of the NFB has shrunk, so it does not attract as much vitriol from the right as the CBC.

The CBC has assumed the role of producing heavily narrated official documentaries, exemplified in monster-house style by the series *Canada: A People's History* (Mark Starowicz, producer, 2001). This seventeen-episode, thirty-two-hour series swallowed so much funding and gathered such ideological backing that it became the new orthodoxy for Canadian history. The series shows how the CBC serves as a mouthpiece for the Canadian state and the official story that the country tells its young people and the world. It also works hard to cover over the difference between the public and the government; the people and the state. *A People's History* attracted a huge audience, 2.6 million viewers per episode, and much critical attention (mostly praise from mainstream reviewers). It was promoted heavily, to a degree rarely seen in Canada, and it involved the most senior producers and managers at the corporation. Its budget of $25 million was so high that it made many other documentary projects impossible for several years. The scale of the series made it, by default, *the* official history for the next generations of students. Another series on this scale will not be possible for twenty to thirty years. [9]

The films in the series are not simple-minded nationalist propaganda. They incorporate much of the criticism directed against previous versions of Canadian history. Moving away from "great men" history, they deal with social and cultural movements, not just politics; they examine the lives and contributions of women, ethnic minorities and ordinary workers; and they include the history of previously overlooked regions. And above all, they deal in a much more nuanced way with the experience of First Nations peoples.

The producers know the language of the new social and political history and the critique from historians on the left, and at times they adopt this language as their own. Elsewhere they subtly debunk it. They call it a "people's history," a history from the bottom up," etc., but as Darrel Varga argues, this is "popular history in an apolitical sense."[10] People's history usually means working-class history and therefore a fundamentally different approach to society. In this series the working-class becomes nothing more than another "special interest."[11] The filmmakers claim that we will not be bored, bamboozled or mystified by professional historians. The message is clear. This is not the dry, elitist history of your grandfather; this is modern, dynamic and exciting. This is not dull academics, it's storytelling, a mode of the people. And they succeeded. Many viewers stated: "I never knew Canadian history was so exciting."

There are other problems. By claiming that this is a history from the bottom-up, showing ordinary people, they imply that we are automatically getting a radically new history. By stating in their promotional material that each segment was directed by a journalist, not a filmmaker, they imply that journalists stick to the truth, they don't fabricate. By replacing historians onscreen with a "voice of God" narrator, they seem to be saying: "Don't worry, we've done the hard and boring work by consulting the historians — we've synthesized everything in a popular way and you'll be spared the academics."

The series doesn't shy from showing problems and tragedies in Canada's past, and this makes it different from most mainstream histories. However, most of these past problems are presented as now resolved. We have moved on. Rick Salutin points to one such example: "The 1837 episode was a Happy Story, as they used to say on *Front Page Challenge.* The rebels started a civil war… but were put down; then Britain sent a nice governor who began political reforms that gave the rebels what they wanted, so-called responsible government. Yet what the rebels said they wanted was full democracy, including independence from the Empire."[12]

In 1992, the CBC attempted to combine the standard essay documentary with something more modern, with actors re-enacting historical events, which blurs the documentary/drama boundaries. But they ran into big trouble. The three-part series *The Valour and the Horror* (1992) by Brian and Terence McKenna, about the Second World War, ran into such strong criticism from veterans groups that the filmmakers were forced to defend themselves before the Senate. The episode that caused the most upset questioned the military tactics of the Allied bombing campaign on Germany. It is difficult to know whether the style of the film or its content alone caused the most trouble. Conservative Senators used the occasion to bash the CBC for its elitist approach, saying that the filmmakers had slandered the veterans. The filmmakers countered that these questions about the war had been raised for years in Britain, Germany and the U.S. Unfortunately, many veterans, not necessarily conservative, felt maligned. Perhaps if the filmmakers had done their homework they would have made a clearer distinction between the military planners and the ordinary air force people who did the fighting.

Another approach to the essay, which historian David Hogarth calls a "middle ground," emerged at the CBC in the 1960s. This retained most of the essay-style characteristics, especially the narration, but emphasized the "actuality value of documentary television." These portraits of Canadian life were "more visual and compelling than anything offered by radio, more neutral and all-seeing than… documentary film and more capable of making sense of the world than any short newscast or live location feed."[13]

Cinema Direct

In the late 1950s, more personal, less official films began to surface at the NFB/ONF and the CBC/ Radio Canada. This paralleled an international trend in documentary toward observation and away from the essay form, but filmmakers in Canada and Quebec made significant contributions in approach and in developing the new light-weight technology that accompanied such films. Terence Macartney-Filgate's *Back-Breaking Leaf* (1959), on tobacco farming, and *Blood and Fire* (1958), on the Salvation Army, both produced in English for the *Candid Eye* series, no longer seemed so tied to a government educational machine.

Some films took critical positions and direct aim at the business and political elites. In particular, the style known as cinema direct,[14] which emerged in Quebec, paralleled the left and liberal facets of the Quiet Revolution then underway. Above all, cinema direct emphasized speech — the ordinary speech of the Québécois. Many filmmakers were not only pro-Quebec but outspoken proponents of the working class. And unlike those working in television, they were not so constrained by the ideology of neutrality. For example, Denys Arcand's *On est au coton* (1970) looked critically at working conditions in Quebec's textile industry. It caused such an uproar among textile manufacturers that the NFB withdrew the film entirely, until 2004. The films of Arthur Lamothe, such as *Le Mépris n'aura qu'un temps* (*Contempt will be short*, 1970), about the deaths of Montreal construction workers, and Gilles Groulx's *24 hours or more* (1973), a "critique of consumer society created by the capitalist system" show that "the point of view of the filmmaker is clearly established, open to discussion and to criticism," say documentary scholars Michel Euvard and Pierre Véronneau. The films "set up before the eyes of the viewer the dialectic of analysis and of reality."[15]

Cinema direct was a true movement. It exhibited not only a style and set of themes but a conscious and vocal intervention into prevailing cinema and the changes underway in Quebec society. Unlike the U.S. style of direct cinema, which favoured a so-called neutral observation, and *cinéma vérité* from France, which interviewed, probed and analyzed in the manner of a social scientist, these new Quebec filmmakers argued that they were part of the community. They would not film from a distance, said Michel Brault, but with a wide-angle, from the middle of the crowd. They also rejected what they called the older folkloric approach, which romanticized traditional Quebec, opting instead for popular culture, unafraid to show urban, contemporary Québécois, warts and all.

Even filmmakers such as Pierre Perrault, who valued the past, were able through cinema direct to show modern people involved with tradition. In his masterpiece, *Pour la suite du monde* (1963), he worked with fishing communities on the St. Lawrence to re-create the past Beluga whale fishing — the result, as photographed by Brault, is stunningly beautiful and moving but not romanticized. Brault was already in demand internationally and played a central role in spreading this style of documentary in the U.S. and France.

The movement around cinema direct also played a role in shaping a major new initiative, known as Challenge for Change/Société nouveau (CFC/SN, 1967–1980), at the NFB/ONF in the 1960s. Under this program, the aims of cinema direct's community development and social change meshed with the ideas of the North American new left. The role of the filmmaker was not to be a neutral observer, nor an independent artist, but rather a participant in change, working alongside communities previously marginalized by society. The Montreal film scholar Tom Waugh believes that by and large the filmmakers working through CFC/SN were not only successful but created a "glittering chunk of the heritage of... bold artistic experimentation and its political dreams of transformation."[16] More than 200 films and tapes were produced, most in the style of cinema direct. This movement was aided by the new technologies of portable video; just as ten years previously cinema direct was partially determined by more portable 16mm film and tape machines. Not all Challenge for Change media employed the style of cinema direct, with some producers opting for the more conventional essay style, which even in these years remained the dominant form for documentary. But cinema direct strongly influenced the philosophy of CFC/SN and to a large extent gave film- and video-makers the methodology for creating dynamic social media.

Independent and Committed

A third significant documentary movement emerged in the 1990s among independent film- and video-makers who wished to combine new styles and technical approaches with more radical politics. These producers often rejected direct ties to the NFB and CBC and the individualist traditions of film and video. Some worked with community or labour organizations, occasionally within the NFB. Canadian documentary producers have never had it easy, but many have successfully cobbled together a mix of funding sources for works largely independent of the state and commercial media. Funding has been provided by arts councils, broadcasters, arms-length government agencies, unions and a myriad of community organizations.

Nine Important Documentary Makers

Hubert Davis, *Invisible City*, 2009
Luc Bourdon, *Memories of Angels*, 2008
John Greyson, *The Fig Trees*, 2009
Ali Kazimi, *Runaway Grooms*, 2005
Brenda Longfellow, *Weather Report*, 2008
Tahani Rached, *Soraida, a Woman of Palestine*, 2004
Laura Sky, *Home Safe Hamilton*, 2010
Min-sook Lee, *Tiger Spirit*, 2008
John Walker, *A Drummer's Dream*, 2010

Immediately obvious with this movement was the ethnic and racial diversity of producers and the large numbers of women involved, especially compared to the demographics at the CBC.

Creative Nonfiction

Print journalists share some of the same forms and approaches as filmmakers or radio producers. For example, there is a broad trend toward storytelling, or creative nonfiction, in journalism. Certainly, the standard hard-news story and the essay-style documentary are by no means dead. Yet, increasingly, we see a merger of reporting with dramatic elements or analysis mixed with personal commentary. In creative nonfiction, dramatic elements include re-created scenes, more focus on individuals, more use of colloquial language and the placing of a reporter or producer in the action. This can blur the boundaries between reporting and opinion, which many readers and viewers find troubling. For example, John Ibbitson's front-page political articles for the *Globe and Mail* mix his conservative views with reporting. However, the lines between reporting and more dramatic elements often remain clear and audiences seem to appreciate the new form — for example, the *Globe*'s features from India by Stephanie Nolen.

Shooting Indians by Ali Kazimi (1997) is a visually fascinating, low-key, almost cerebral documentary, which exemplifies the creative nonfiction trend. It tells the story of Kazimi's friendship with Jeffery Thomas, a First Nations photographer whose life has seen some ups and downs. Together they wrestle with questions over the representations of Aboriginal people in Canadian photography, past and present. The film unfolds through first-person narration from Kazimi's experience as an Asian Indian-Canadian working with a Canadian Indian. The film holds our attention partly because it tells a story — we're not sure how Thomas's life will turn out. In fact, the film was abandoned for some years because things weren't going well. In the end, viewers see that Thomas has become a superb artist and now works at Canada's National Archives. The film also succeeds because we can see the connection between the filmmaker and his subject and because Kazimi uses a first-person approach to explore many complex issues.

Carts of Darkness (2008) by Murray Siple shows another kind of creative nonfiction:

A close-up of a shopping cart
A city street on a hill rushing past — a point-of-view shot from in the cart
The image is bouncing wildly — up and down
Shouts — laughing — bits of fear in the voice
Incredible noise of hard wheels and metal — bouncing along a road at high speed.

We're participating in a filmmaker's wild ride in a shopping cart with no brakes down a steep hill in Vancouver. Murray Siple is performing a scene in his film about homeless men who collect bottles and ride carts for thrills. The title suggests Joseph Conrad's famous novel of Africa, *Heart of Darkness.* It's partly a joke. But Siple's title also suggests that he will be exploring an underground, sometimes dark, world of the homeless. These include physical and mental hardship, alienation, addiction and sometimes despair. As the film reaches its conclusion we learn also that Siple was once a dare-devil snowboarder who became severally crippled. His story, he implies, parallels theirs.

But *Carts of Darkness* shows both the positive and negative aspects of a personalized, storytelling documentary. It allows Siple to bring viewers into the action and give us additional ways of understanding the men he hangs out with. He is also able to get closer to the men — he wants to connect, not simply document or record their activities. And yet, there's a touch of creepiness to the scenes of interaction between filmmaker and his subjects. Is it ethical to encourage the men to play these dangerous games? Is it reasonable to equate the life of a middle-class filmmaker (regardless of his disability) with the lives of homeless men with no money, power or connections? I'm not saying that Siple is out of bounds, only that these are the risks of getting close to a film's subjects and of emphasizing dangerous antics for the sake of entertainment. Will audiences remember the wild cart races or the complexities of their life situations and loneliness?

Film and TV Drama

By the mid-1950s, Canadian television had carved out distinctive forms of drama in both TV series and episodes within anthologies. And, in the period since 1970, Canada has developed a somewhat stable film industry. Films such as *Goin' Down the Road* (1970) by Don Shebib, set in east-end Toronto, and *The Rowdyman* (1971) by Peter Carter, in working-class St. John's, go out of their way to show the influence of place, history and geography on the characters and the stories. Like most realist films the style is low-key and doesn't call attention to itself; the stories contain some ups and downs but nothing you might call high drama. The characters speak in their particular accents. The mood is decidedly down-beat. Two early influential films, *Nobody Waved Goodbye* (Don Owen, 1964) and *Le chat dans le sac* (Gilles Groulx, 1964), used an observational documentary style to create a realist atmosphere. But, as mentioned earlier, realism hardly describes the entire range of drama.

Some films originally discussed as realist because their settings were specifically Canadian now appear greatly stylized or intensely dramatic. William Fruet's *Wedding in White* (1972) displays minutely detailed sets and props from the Second World War, but the staging and drama are so intensely theatrical as to be far removed from realism. The much admired hit *Mon oncle Antoine* (Claude Jutra and Michel Brault, 1971), which faithfully depicts a Quebec mining district in the 1940s, also includes strong doses of fantasy and romanticism, not entirely in line with straight realism. It's a stronger film for it.

Instead of realism, it's better to think in terms of three broad streams of dramatic fiction. The first stream closely resembles the dominant genres of U.S. and international cinema and TV — comedy, action, romance and horror. These productions sit squarely within the most formulaic elements of their genres in narrative form, style and content. They include *Porky's* (1982), *Meatballs* (1979), *Black Christmas* (1974), *A History of Violence* (2005), *Being Erica* (2009–) and *Flashpoint*, among hundreds of others. Often it's not possible to distinguish between these Canadian works and low-budget U.S. productions being shot here to take advantage of tax breaks and lower costs. This does not mean that the films don't reflect how and where they were made. Most use smaller budgets and Canadian actors, usually unknown to an international audience. The key elements for popular and financial success are the genre elements plus the quality of script and acting.

Over the years these films have been controversial because some of them are clearly low budget and bad. When public money has been spent, it makes the situation worse. But even with high-quality work, critics often fault the films because they don't reflect Canada and Canadian values (a slippery term to define). "What's the point," Canadian nationalists say, "of spending all that money if the films don't advance Canada's standing in the world?" To complicate matters, some of these productions are generic thrillers or slashers that nevertheless flaunt their Canadian content — thus falling in the cultural cringe category.

The second stream includes prestige productions, usually completed with government funds or broadcasting money. These generally include some combination of Canadian content, actors, writers and directors and have higher budgets for both production and distribution. A key difference from the U.S. lookalikes is that Canadian locations are not hidden or are even obvious. Vancouver is clearly Vancouver, not a stand-in for Seattle. Most of these fit within the recognizable genres of family-adventure, war, crime, legal drama or ensemble situation comedy. Well-known examples include *The Beachcombers* (1972–1990), *Anne of Green Gables* (1985), *Passchendaele* (2008), *Away from Her* (2006), *DaVinci's Inquest* (1998–2005), *The Border, Polytechnique* (2009), *Corner Gas* and *Little Mosque on the Prairie*.

Many historical dramas fall into this category as well, some based on actual events and characters, such as *Bethune: The Making of a Hero* (1992), *Dieppe* (1993), *The Rocket* (2005); others set in the past but with fictional characters and situations (*Anne of Green Gables* [1985], *Maria Chapdelaine* [1984]). Among my earliest TV memories in this vein were two CBC efforts, *Radisson* (1957–58) and *The Last of the Mohicans* (1957–58), starring the amazingly old and wise Lon Chaney Jr. as Chingachgook.

Working within Hollywood genres does not, of course, rule out thought-provoking, far-reaching drama. And CBC TV does have an older tradition of critical drama, unafraid of prevailing ideologies. Peter Pearson's *Tar Sands*, from 1983, stands out as a work that touched raw nerves in the oil patch and the government of Alberta. An older series, *Wojeck* (1966–67), attracted plenty of viewers and good critical attention. The show, starring John Vernon as Toronto's chief coroner, was a "message drama, not preachy but certainly laden with meaning," says TV historian Paul Rutherford.[17] It used "the saga to dramatize such public issues as the generation gap, the profit motive, and the new morality to disturb comfortable views and awaken the public conscience to the wrongs around them." One episode tackled racism and featured the jailhouse suicide of a young Aboriginal man from Moosonee. Authentic locations such as Spadina's Silver Dollar tavern gave the stories a solid base of realism, but the cinematography also captured moods of characters and settings as well. The series overall reached 2.5 million viewers. Rutherford wisely reminds us however that although the acting, photography and dialogue were top notch, the genre conventions of an "embattled professional" in a nice package shine through. Occasionally a prestige production straddles the boundaries of low-brow genre fiction and unabashed Canadiana, such as Bruce McDonald's *Hard Core Logo* (2006) and his horror film *Pontypool* (2009). Of course, prestige is a loaded term, and many cultural bureaucrats may have difficulty following McDonald everywhere he'd like to go. But most of his later work has received the money and blessings of Telefilm Canada.

The third stream falls within the genre of the art film. These are made for specialized cinema audiences at festivals and in theatres. They rarely turn up on TV. Art films have many of the following characteristics:

- a notable director's style;
- a mixing of genres or genre conventions, such as comedy and crime;
- complex characters and settings;
- ensemble casts rather than a single protagonist;
- open-ended, more difficult or challenging plots; and
- different styles or rhythms of editing from those of mainstream Hollywood.

Atom Egoyan's *The Sweet Hereafter* (1996) was voted by film industry followers in 2002 as the best Canadian film ever (which I wouldn't dispute). Although Egoyan's most accessible work, it will unfortunately continue to search for a sizeable audience by mainstream standards. Similarly, Denys Arcand's *The Decline of the American Empire* (1986) and *Jesus of Montreal* (1989) did well financially in the international market but remain art films in Canada.

Schools for the Stars

Colm Feore (b. 1958) – National Theatre School in Montreal "I do dead Canadians. If he's dead and he's Canadian and he's famous I'll be playing him at some point."
Brent Butt (b. 1966) – Yuk Yuks Comedy Club
Sarah Polley (b. 1979) – showbiz family, first role at four years old, Toronto's Claude Watson School for the Performing Arts, in the Toronto District Board of Education
Adam Beach (b. 1972) – Manitoba Theatre for Young People
Megan Follows (b. 1968) – showbiz family, TV commercials, starting at nine
Roy Dupuis (b. 1963) – National Theatre School in Montreal
Genevieve Bujold (b. 1942) – Montréal Conservatoire d'Art Dramatique
Zaib Shaikh (b. 1974) – plays Amaar Rashid in *Little Mosque on the Prairie*, University of Toronto and Sheridan College theatre schools.

Some art films crossover to a larger audience, moving from the independent, art cinema into the mainstream and generating good box-office as well as critical reception. The best-known recent example is *Water* by Deepa Mehta (2006). This exquisitely beautiful film set in 1940s India takes us deep into a closed world, showing the horrific treatment of child brides abandoned by society when their husbands die. The film displays most of the characteristics of an international art film, using a mix of genres, an ensemble cast, complex characters, etc., though its editing and scene construction stay close to more conventional patterns. *Water* also represents a newer dimension of Canadian film — an Indian story told by a Canadian of Indian descent — an historical story of importance to many Indo-Canadians today. Its prestige international cast gives it weight and credibility in both India and Canada.[18]

Other art films clearly aim for a specialized audience. As an analogy think of the difference between the literary fiction of Margaret Atwood and the mass market science fiction of Robert Sawyer or any Harlequin romance. With Atom Egoyan it can take a while before realizing you have plunged into a different movie-world experience. With Guy Maddin you know you're not in Brampton anymore right off the bat; oddly beautiful, strange, creepy, absurd, abstract, surrealist and funny are words that come to mind when watching *My Winnipeg* (2007) or the brilliant *Tales from the Gimli Hospital* (1988), which launched his fame. The avant-garde theatre informs the work of several other art filmmakers, especially Quebec's Lea Pool and Robert Lepage, in films both cerebral and challenging for most audiences. Performance art, avant-garde video, the political manifesto, gay pornography and a wicked sense of humour help define John Greyson's work. His best-known film is *Lillies* (1996), based on a play, but he works equally well in short didactic videos and computer-based image creations that make remarkable, thought-provoking links between AIDS, African liberation struggles, the plight of Palestinians in Gaza, absurd Canadian politicians. He is a leading voice of queer activism in Canada, a regular award winner at the Berlin Film Festival and much more.

The Model from the South

The influence of U.S. culture affects Canadian media-making as well, often in ways that aren't obvious. For example, many Canadian films, TV shows and musical forms take their cue from U.S. genres, styles and trends. Even when Canadian producers succeed in creating different forms they know their work will be measured by audiences and critics against the dominant forms and will often be found wanting simply because they depart from the norms. Canadians can never raise the amounts of money needed to compete within some genres, especially the spectacles of action, adventure, science fiction and feature-length animation. Thus, Canadians have generally concentrated on other forms and genres, usually ones that involve realism or styles not particularly damaged by low budgets. This state of affairs need not lead to a crisis of quality, but for many Canadian audiences it sets the stage for disappointment, lack of interest and failure.

"We're not asking for a lot here," said actor Nicholas Campbell. "I don't think it's too much to ask that Canadians can see two hours

Canada's Popular Programs	
Drama	**Téléroman**
1950s — *Kraft Television Theatre, The Plouffe Family*	*La famille Plouffe*
1960s — *Wojeck, Cariboo Country*	*D'Iberville*
1970s — *The Beachcombers, A Gift to Last*	*Duplessis*
1980s — *Street Legal, Night Heat*	*Lance et Compte (He Shoots, He Scores)*
1990s — *DaVinci's Inquest*	*Rene Levesque (series)*
2000s — *Intelligence, The Border*	*Les Boys/Belle Baie*
Comedy and Variety	
1950s — *The Big Review*	*Porte ouverte*
1960s — *Wayne and Shuster, Music Hop, Razzle Dazzle, Music Hall*	
1970s — *Don Messer's Jubilee, The Tommy Hunter Show*	
1980s — *Second City Television (SCTV)*	
1990s — *The Newsroom*	*Un Gars, une fille*
2000s — *Little Mosque on the Prairie, 22 Minutes*	*Star Academy, Le coeur a ses raisons (soap parody)*
News and Public Affairs	
1950s — *Tabloid, Close-up*	*Point de mire*
1960s — *This Hour Has Seven Days, Telescope*	*Le Telejournal (continuing)*
1970s — *Fifth estate, W5 (both continuing)*	

1980s — *The Journal, The Nature of Things* (continuing), *The Ten Thousand Day War*	
1990s — CBC Newsworld channel launched	*Le Point*
2000s — *The Hour* (G. Stroumboulopoulos)	*Enquete/Dumont 360*

of our own original, scripted programming in prime time a week."[19] At the same press conference in 2009 where Campbell spoke, other actors and their representatives pointed out that Canadian English-language drama has been "a rarity in prime time" since 1999, when the CRTC (Canadian Radio-Television and Telecommunications Commission) relaxed Canadian content rules. Since then, "Canadian private broadcasters have been saturating Canada's prime time schedules with U.S. shows." In 2008 they spent $740 million on U.S. and foreign programming and just $54 million on Canadian English-language drama and comedies.[20]

Television News

Television roared across Canada in 1952 with a speed and power unmatched by any media before or since. Even the personal computer and internet, spoken of today as revolutionary, pales in comparison. The box was absolutely fascinating. It was also relatively cheap, and within fifteen years it had infiltrated nearly every Canadian home.

By 1954, CBC Television was presenting a fifteen-minute national newscast. On the English side the presenter was Larry Henderson, a former reporter and Shakespearean actor. Henderson and his producers knew that delivery was key — how you read the news was very important. He was the voice of authority — and of the entire corporation. The producers had three models to draw from: BBC TV, the U.S. TV networks and CBC Radio. At first it was radio that played the biggest role, but as the first years went by, TV people learned that pictures were essential. For many the motto became: no pictures, no story. But TV production cost a fortune compared to radio and took far more people. In 1952 the CBC employed about 1,400 people; by 1959 there were 7,000.

TV was born during the biggest economic boom ever. Not only did millions buy the sets, but advertisers knew a bonanza when they saw one. One station owner said that the advertisers were "insatiable." This was the result of a government decision to follow the U.S. rather than the British model, so that CBC TV would have to rely on advertising for a good portion of its budget. U.S. TV manufacturers liked the prospects too. Chicago's Admiral company set up shop in Port Credit, just west of Toronto, in "a shiny brick-and-glass structure on the mud flats," said *Time* magazine, and by 1951 they were selling more than 25,000 sets a year — that's one year before Canadian TV got started. "U.S. business has recognized that Canada is still a great industrial frontier," said the *Time* writer.[21]

The country's intellectual elites also nurtured high hopes for TV. One member of the Massey Commission in the early 1950s stated that Canadian culture was "an embarrassment" and that "it looked like we were a nation of barbarians." TV, they hoped, would do what radio had failed to do — create a genuine Canadian culture of a high standard and clearly different from the U.S. mainstream.[22]

Like the BBC, Canada's leading news shows have run in mid- to late-evening slots. This reflects their importance and perhaps the lack of genuinely popular prime-time shows. The only programming that has disrupted their schedules has been NHL hockey, by far the most popular Canadian TV. In terms of quality — its scope, depth, professional standards, independence and diversity — Canadian TV news sits squarely between the highs of the BBC and the lows of the U.S. networks. Competition for CBC's prime news programs now comes from the private groups: CTV, which became a national network in 1961, and Global, formed in the 1980s. Their broadcasts are similar, although Global spends less, and the results are obvious.

The similar approach makes it common practice for journalists and anchors to move from one network to another.

Reporters and Readers

In its first programs, CBC TV news began life as nothing much more than a radio script read by the serious and temperamental Larry Henderson sitting formally behind a desk. The newsreader, presenter or anchor remains a key element in TV news. Over the years stations have experimented with every kind of news desk, camera angle and framing strategy. For some newscasts, the anchor now leaves the desk and stands for key moments or even the entire program. Regardless of the set-up, the most important element is the authority of the anchor. After all, anchors represent the station, the network and journalism in general. They are the face that legitimizes the news organization in its role as "fourth estate," equivalent to other groups in society. Larry Henderson wasn't what you'd call glamourous. Today, the anchor must be likeable, telegenic, acceptable to sponsors and a magnet for high ratings.

The Museum of Broadcast Communications in Chicago has this to say about the CBC's veteran anchor Peter Mansbridge: "Mansbridge's style of presentation is understated and sober, but sufficiently amiable to attract viewers in the increasingly entertainment-oriented news media. This understated delivery, in combination with his appearance — once described as 'bland good looks' — makes Mansbridge's presentation and persona consistent with the standard among Canadian broadcast journalists."[23] This sober and amiable look nets Peter Mansbridge a salary of $280,000. (If this seems high, the CBC believes that its hockey star Don Cherry rates $750,000 for performing his cock-of-the-walk for ten minutes during the second intermission).

The only other people in TV news with the visual status to approach the audience head-on are the reporters, who have the same type of authority as the anchors. Anyone else on camera, even important news-makers, must look slightly off-camera or speak sideways to a reporter. Reporters rank second only to the anchor as the public face of the news organization. TV news organizations go to great lengths to build up the image of their reporters. They don't need to be as photogenic as the anchors, and sometimes a weather-beaten appearance adds street credibility, but generally reporters look good on camera, sporting stylish hair and perfect teeth. Ads and slogans for the news department promote the reporters' work and push them forward as celebrity professionals. Anchors and key reporters regularly fly off on prestige field assignments (dangerous but not too dangerous) to display their journalist skills. Donning a flak jacket and jeans and cutting back on the make-up helps show their seriousness. Everyone works hard to refute the popular notion that the anchor is just a pretty face, not a real journalist.

Back in the studio, sets have evolved from bare and drab back-drops to elaborate, over-the-top theatrical productions. Even small-scale local news programs like to show off their set and production facilities. The scale of the set seems to reflect the resources of the station and its connection to a vast electronic world of news-gathering. A back wall of TV monitors and international clocks is a favourite design, with numerous people hurrying past in the background to give the feeling of perpetual activity. The news never stops. Viewers never see people just sitting at desks and writing scripts. That would imply that the news is a created product rather than a series of constantly breaking outside events.

In 2009, the CBC news programs changed their look rather dramatically so that everyone now stands, including the anchor, in-studio quests and reporters. This generated much mirth and some scorn. Many viewers felt the CNN style was not the right direction for the CBC. "Fact is," says, John Doyle, the *Globe and Mail*'s feisty TV critic "CBC News has contorted itself in order to appear more popu-list, mainstream and appealing to everyone. It has been terrorized into avoiding any appearance of political bias. That is why Pastor Mansbridge stands around to deliver the news on *The National*, like a friendly fella hoping to see a friendly face and have a nice chinwag.

That's why there's all that absurd chumminess on *The National*. Like when the Pastor talks to Neil Macdonald and they end up going, 'Neil,' 'Peter,' 'Neil,' 'Peter,' saying each other's names over and over."[24]

Local News

Local TV news has suffered in North America and Britain since the 2008 economic crisis. But the cuts to staff, programs and even stations stretches back many years. In Canada, for instance, major cuts accompanied the recessions of 1994, 2000 and 2009. Local news shows take national or international stories and find the local angle. Or editors dig up a local story that they hope will get picked up by a network. But their mandate centres on the content — local above all.

The success of a local program depends greatly on its studio talent. Local newscasters almost never present stories on their own. They're part of a team. A man and woman read the main news, accompanied by the quirky weather person, the fast-talking jock and the bubbly favourite who covers entertainment. The show features a lot of light-hearted joking and kidding. Sometimes the banter sets the scene for a little flirting, where the man and woman play the roles of a familiar, but not married, couple. TV's *Breakfast Television* takes these antics the furthest. This chemistry, or lack of it, quickly gets translated into ratings and affects the advertising money.

Local news often tries to strike a different tone from the national news. Rather than focusing on the tragic, the scary, the bewildering and the bad, local news regularly produces "good news" stories or "happy news." Although this style is most obvious in the U.S., it exists in a milder form in Canada. To some extent happy news responds to audience surveys that complain that the news is "too depressing" or "the media are just too cynical." In trying to answer these critiques happy news often comes across as trite entertainment. Cities have serious problems with massive poverty, injustice and oppression. Happy news ignores all that. Local news viewers experience far less turnover of reporters and anchors than at the networks. A familiar face reads the news every night, in many cases for decades. When everything else in the world, including the news business, is changing rapidly, the local news faces provide a steady, neighbourly presence — like a family that's lived in the area for thirty years.

Local news loves the slogan, "news you can use." Of course, reporting the news in a way that makes connections between the story and the viewers' lives is effective and informative. For example, a story about a local refugee family can be expanded to explain where the family has come from and why they are fleeing. Conversely, a big world event that takes place in India can be the occasion to introduce viewers to local Indian communities. In Canada this slogan often masquerades as a general critique, especially in the West, of the CBC, that it spends too much time on Ottawa politics and the Toronto elites.

The problem with "news you can use," as with the happy news phenomenon, is that too often it becomes an excuse to bury one's head in the sand, sticking to the local when the community desperately needs a wider perspective. Much of this parochial news centres on lifestyle or consumer issues — how to buy a car, new fads in health care or nifty home renovations. A steady diet of these issues, to the exclusion of the more traditional hard news, means that citizens lack the information they need to participate in a true democracy. For example, in the area of public health a local news show might report unusually high cancer rates in one neighbourhood but neglect to investigate further. If they did they might find similar problems in other parts of the country and become aware of patterns or see that a known industrial polluter once operated near their area.

Current Affairs Radio

There are two kinds of current affairs radio (one might be tempted to call them sober and drunk). The first type includes discussions and interviews, some light and chatty, others sober and pitched to an informed audience. The second type, called talk radio, uses a call-in format, strong opinions and very short calls.

CBC/Radio Canada offers programming in English, French and eight Aboriginal languages on its domestic radio service; in nine languages on its international radio service, Radio Canada International; and in eight languages on its web-based radio service, RCI Viva, a service for recent and aspiring immigrants to Canada. Most educated, middle-class Canadians prefer the news and current affairs offered on CBC Radio to anything else. If we agree with polls that show the majority of Canadians share attitudes and ideas of the centre-left, say from Jack Layton to David Suzuki, CBC Radio is the place to go. My sense, without a scientific analysis, is that a majority of hosts and employees there would vote Liberal, NDP or Green. In the eyes of the right, it's a nest of communists.

Current affairs programming at CBC Radio follows a magazine format, which means it includes a variety of items of varying length, separated by bits of music (usually instrumental). Included in this category are prestige interview shows such as *As it Happens*, hosted by the excellent Carol Off, and *The Current* with Anna Maria Tremonti. The hosts are experienced journalists, well-informed and well-prepared. Guests are invariably articulate, and long-form interviews cover international and national stories. Regional programs feature the same format but use a more eclectic mix of interviews, from serious to fluffy, and cover some regional news stories. Compared to TV fare, these daytime shows are much more sober, but like their TV cousins, they strain to interact with their audience — often through contests, witty letter readings and call-ins.

Sunday Edition, with its host Michael Enright, also ranks high in prestige. Enright positively glows with upper-crust culture, the kind of fellow those Canadian elites of the 1950s had in mind to raise the taste of the masses. But the show and its predecessor, *Sunday Morning,* can also point to a long history of radio documentary, much of which has been excellent, perhaps especially the work of Bob Carty. For example, the show for August 22, 2010, featured Camilla Gibb speaking about her new literary novel, *The Beauty of Humanity Movement,* the roots of its inspiration in Vietnam and where she's heading as a writer. Also featured was Karin Wells's feature documentary, *The Women Are Coming*, a "look back at the day in May 1970 when a caravan of women took over the House of Commons — an act of civil disobedience that helped change this country's abortion laws."

The long-running documentary and interview program *Dispatches* airs weekly. Here's how their website describes what they do: "Dispatches is a hybrid program. It's got a foot in the daily news agenda, but doesn't follow it. It's got a foot in the considered world of current affairs, the arts and features. That gives reporters great scope in pitching. We listen to topical pitches with a news peg, or something out of the blue that may not be on anyone's agenda yet."

Talk radio projects an entirely different sense of the country. It is dominated by right-wing hosts, apparently unafraid of making their views known. It's the home of backlash, anger and ignorance. Some hosts qualify as knowledgeable and serious, such as Rex Murphy and Michael Coren. Others are windbags — rude and arrogant. At most times there is little real discussion; rather, the shows take the form of hurling insults, interrupting, and ad hominem jabs. No one gets more than a few seconds to state an opinion before the host jumps in. Many of these hosts see themselves as mavericks in the media world, their mission: to channel the common sense of real people. Craig Chandler, for example, of Freedom Radio Network, in Alberta, likes the motto: "Hard hitting, truthful radio." They love to shock and attack what they call political correctness — this translates as backlash media against women, immigrants, Native people and minorities of all kinds. Their idols, even in Quebec, are the U.S. shock jocks Don Imus and Howard Stern.

Unless you share the views of the host and callers, this qualifies as the most depressing media in the country. You hear more knowledgeable and civilized conversation in the average bar. An Ottawa radio station describes their man Lowell Green's latest book as "a testament to Lowell's deeply held convictions about what he calls, 'the defining social policies of Canadian life.'" The station describes his book like this: "How the Granola Crunching, Cappuccino Sucking,

Tree Hugging, Thug Huggers are Ruining this Country is a well-researched look at such issues as needle exchange programs, crime, recycling, global warming, and Canada's refugee policies."[25]

The Daily Newspaper

The newspaper still rules as the most reliable source of news, with the most extensive coverage, for most Canadians. In total there are eighty-five English and eleven French language daily papers. Every day more than 4.1 million Canadians purchase a newspaper; that's 26.9 million copies in an average week. This does not even measure readers, only buyers, and doesn't include all those who read the eighteen free dailies.[26]

Newspapers still devote far more time to original news-gathering than any other media. That's one reason why the current problems, such as job cuts for thousands of journalists, attract so much attention. Newspaper coverage in general compared to other news media is broader and deeper, and newspapers still employ a far greater proportion of full-time journalists. Consequently, TV and radio broadcasting, as well as the internet, remain dependent on stories generated by newspapers.

Newspaper purchases have declined in North America and parts of Western Europe — in Canada a drop of 4 percent from 2008 to 2009; in the U.S. a drop of 5 percent from 2002 to 2007, to 52 million daily copies; and in Germany a drop of 2 percent, to 21 million copies. And yet, even in the U.S., where papers have suffered in the economic crisis, newspaper advertising has grown into a $40 billion business. That's twice as big as it was twenty years ago.[27] So the newspaper industry worldwide seems pretty healthy, despite the doom and gloom in some quarters.

For their owners, newspapers continue to provide considerable political power as well, because Canada's elites in business and government look to the major papers more than other media forms. When the journalist Peter Newman questioned John Bassett, the owner of the *Toronto Evening Telegram*, if he "used his paper to attack his foes and praise his friends, John Bassett asked with genuine astonishment, 'Why else would I own one?'"[28] Newman also interviewed David Radler, who worked closely for thirty-five years with the jailed tycoon Conrad Black. Radler put it this way. "I will ultimately determine what the newspapers say and how they're going to be run. If editors disagree with us, they should disagree with us when they're no longer in our employ."

The Future of Newspapers

Many casual observers of the Canadian media believe that newspapers are doomed. They see a major crisis because, they say, the business model, based on advertising, seems broken. We've heard non-stop wailing and moaning from groups who love papers and from those who loath them. But this talk centres entirely on the short-term difficulties in the big, dominant media. In the U.S. especially, we've seen constant predictions about newspapers about to crash or companies sliding into bankruptcy. Some pundits in 2009 actually predicted the end of the *New York Times*.

In Canada, we've heard a similar ruckus, especially since the CanWest Global empire imploded. It's the same in Britain, exemplified by the sorry state of the *Independent* newspaper group, which was sold in 2010. But so much of this is exaggeration: first off, very few papers have actually disappeared — even with the Tribune Company, which owns the *Chicago Tribune* and the *LA Times*, the papers have continued despite the parent's bankruptcy problems.

There have been changes of owners and lower profits (but in the U.S. on average still above 10 percent), and there has been a shift to internet delivery for some content and advertising. But none of this indicates the death of newspapers. What's happening is a return to more stable management and a retreat from the reckless, cowboy capitalism practiced by the media parent companies, which precipitated the crisis. But throughout all this, the news business itself has remained profitable. For example, the Chicago real estate developer

Sam Zell used $8 billion in borrowed money to take over the Tribune Company in 2007 (only a portion devoted to news).[29] His stupendous fall into the red in 2008 should have been predictable, just like the U.S. housing mortgage collapse. As for *The Independent* in the U.K., its situation was not bad enough to prevent a bidding war to buy it, including a £1 billion offer from the Stern Group of Germany. [30]

Types of Newspapers

Most news vendors in major cities of the world sell what are known as broadsheets and tabloids. Throughout the twentieth century, the "quality" papers were called broadsheets because of their width and their length, which requires a fold. The news term "above the fold" refers to important stories on the top half of the page. The first priority for these papers was, and remains, the coverage of politics, economics and world issues. They still appeal to avid readers among the ruling elites and middle class and continue to exert significant political influence.

The lowly tabloid — a word derived from the brand-name "condensed tablet," a nineteenth-century term for mass-produced pills — scorned by elites and intellectuals, is half the size of a broad-

Broadsheets and Tabloids	
Canadian Broadsheets ("Quality") Papers	Canadian Tabloids
eighty in total	sixteen in total
Le Devoir	Toronto *Sun*, Vancouver *Sun*, Winnipeg *Sun*, etc.
Globe and Mail	Journal de Montreal
Toronto Star	*Metro* (various cities)
National Post	*24* (Toronto)
Montreal *Gazette*	*The Province* (B.C.)
Fredericton *Daily Gleaner*	

sheet, with no fold. Tabloids provide condensed news. Right from the start, these papers rolled out a simplified and cruder journalism, often focused on scandal and sensationalism. In general their readers are less well-educated, poorer and less influential. Tabloids also incorporate much louder and more garish advertising.

News stories differ to some extent in the two types of papers. Most tabloid stories are short, with clipped sentences and plain language. Often they consist of only a dozen paragraphs, all composed of one or two sentences. The stories usually fit on one page, which eliminates the need to flip ahead, and their design looks increasingly like magazines, with no stories whatsoever on the front page.

Hard News

Hard news stories can either be based on a response to events or employ an active approach. They start with a "lead" — a sentence or paragraph that lays out, right away, the five Ws — the what, where, who, when and why. From that beginning, the story resembles an inverted pyramid. It spells out the most vital information at the top and provides the least important near the end. According to this model, readers who want only the basic information will find it in the first two or three paragraphs. Others can stick with it to learn more and more specific or minor details. This model allows editors to easily cut the item for length, starting at the bottom. It also allows the quickest and most flexible means of translation to another medium, say from print to a website. A ten-paragraph newspaper item might get chopped to twenty words in a text message.

Reporters write these items in the third person and never refer to themselves. The idea is to present the story in a form that looks as objective and unbiased as possible. There is much to be said for this clear, direct style. But language always carries other meanings. In this case the implication is that the content is true and that no one appears to have selected or shaped the story. In hard news stories, descriptions of people and settings only appear if they are essential to the story. They always mention the date and place. And increasingly, because of twenty-four-hour all-news delivery, they indicate the exact time that an event took place and when the story was posted or written. In the old days reporters could use the past tense, but competition from TV, radio and the web have forced a more immediate writing style. Now you read "Car bomb kills 10 in Baghdad," "Business leaders meet to discuss…"

Reporters follow many basic routines in news-gathering and writing up these stories. Statements from news-makers or eye-witnesses always get written up in quotation marks. ("The mayor is just trying to line his pockets," says a local business-owner.) This makes the story feel "true" and protects the journalist. By putting questionable, biased or outrageous statements in quotes, the journalist can liven up the story and appear to be simply passing on one person's view. These quotations usually get balanced with others that take a different or conflicting view. (In reply, the mayor stated, "I never made a penny on those deals.") This charge and counter-charge format allows the reporter to claim that a story is balanced and unbiased.

Features

Feature writing gives journalists an opportunity to write longer stories and to delve into the background or context. Although features deal with current events, the time-frame is often extended. Features provide readers with more of the "whys" behind a news story or explain the significance of events. In addition, features are not locked into any particular style. Sometimes they delay the lead and start instead with an anecdote, sketching in a setting or describing a person. This "soft lead" style appears increasingly in hard-news stories as well. Features often read like short stories, making ample use of narrative devices. For instance, they might withhold information, create conflict, follow one person, build to a climax or end with a "kicker" — a surprising or shocking ending.

Many features don't simply describe, they establish a scene. This follows the general trend toward creative nonfiction. In addition to using narrative and drama, creative nonfiction brings the thoughts and feelings of the writer into the story. This never happens in the hard news approach. Editors usually vary the types of features they run. Personality profiles mix interview and observation as well as creative writing and editorializing. Human interest stories and trend stories deal with everything from popular fads to suggestions for better ways to live. In-depth stories use research and recap major news. A backgrounder or analysis piece fills out the context of a current issue.

Images

Just as literacy and the power of the text have expanded worldwide so has the proliferation of images, above all through the news media. Without the power and immediacy of photographs, could the news media remain a mass medium? I doubt it. Most of us would take much less interest if the news did not include photography. It is photography that delivers the audience to advertisers. *The Canadian Press Stylebook* points out: "A good picture can carry a story onto page one; lack of a picture can take a good story... right out of the paper."[31]

Machine-based images, in contrast with their hand-drawn predecessors, carry the authority of truth. Even though we know that photographs can be doctored, we still fall into the belief that the mechanical image does not lie. For that reason photographs go hand-in-hand with the mythology of a professional, objective point of view. Photography also broadens the news agenda, bringing us into contact with everyday events and ordinary people. It can show us the details of settings and places as well as moods, relationships and feelings. Unlike nineteenth-century newspapers, papers no longer focus exclusively on the doings of the rich and powerful.

Non-News

News makes up, on average, only 40 percent of newspaper content. Some papers carry much less. The ads alone gobble up a huge proportion of space, charging at us in three basic forms: display ads, classified ads and ads masquerading as stories. The story-form ads usually appear in the fashion, auto, technology, real estate and lifestyle sections. They're basically product promotions with photos supplied by the seller and with text only slightly rewritten from press releases. For example, a survey of world newspapers in March 2008 shows dozens with front-page stories, complete with colour pictures, of the newly released Apple iPhone. The insider term for this kind of journalism, where writers churn out rewrites of press releases, is "churnalism."

One Chicago editor lets us in on another priority: "We made sure we sailed the seven C's. The seven C's that help build habits: Columnists, Crosswords, Classified, Comics, Celebrity, Channels [TV listings], Color [like the weather page]!"[32]

This reference to building habits should remind us that modern news media need us to keep coming back — tomorrow or to the next edition or the next hour. They work hard to develop our brand loyalty, a practice that shapes many news genres. We know their slogans by heart: stay tuned, join us tonight, sign up for our news-feed, keep it locked.

Journalism students at San José State University in California have quantified many of these trends, including the use of superficial stories and non-news, on a website called Grade the News. In a 2006 report they conclude, "After watching more than a thousand TV stories, our overall impression was that local stations are extremely good at covering the least important news of the day — random action events such as episodes of violence, fires and accidents."[33]

Headlines

One of the most valued skills in a newsroom is the ability to write headlines. A copy-editor, not the reporter, usually performs this role and provides some continuity of style throughout the paper. A good headline keeps it "simple and direct," says journalism professor Malcolm Gibson. "Do not," he says, "editorialize, exaggerate, generalize."[34] Unfortunately, this advice to students gets rough treatment in the newsroom. Headlines often suggest in a subtle (or

---

Seven Spinning Headlines (August 26, 2010)

"PM steals show with impromptu dance" —Montreal *Gazette*
"Harper dances with Inuvialuit performers" —*Toronto Star*
"PM shimmies, shouts as he joins Inuit dance group" —*CTV.ca*
"Harper boogies in the Arctic" —*Globe and Mail*
"Harper Dances in Northwest Territories" —*580 CFRA Radio*
"Harper goes native with dance moves" —*Toronto Sun*
"Who would win a dance-off — Stephen Harper or Vladimir Putin?"
—*National Post*

---

not so subtle) way how the reader should interpret the news story below. It's a form of masked editorializing that reflects the editor's or owner's point of view and signals a paper's identity or brand image. The Sun chain of papers specialize in witty but usually slanted and misleading headlines. "Leaf in nude photo flap," "Roid rage? Drugs found in wrestler's home after murder-suicide." "We've been duped by the Tamils."

The tabloids love brash phrases: "It may shock you, but it must be told!" A headline can use puns or alliteration to turn a straight news story into a joke. It can also personalize an issue, even when the reporter has taken pains not to. For example, a reporter may have covered a farm community meeting and noted that many people expressed opinions. But the headline simplifies and personalizes things by announcing, "Brown triumphs over Trembley in close vote." Headlines often emphasize conflict and flatten complex stories into sensational catch phrases.

3. THE BIG ISSUES

Diversity

Diversity stands out as the number one issue facing Canadian society and its media. This is a multi-racial, multi-ethnic, multi-lingual country, accompanied by vast regional differences. We need media of all kinds in order to facilitate communication among so many groups. Historically, the government made it a priority to address regional issues by promoting universal access to basic communication. This was exemplified in the nineteenth century with the creation of cross-country telegraph, rail and postal systems. Similarly, in the twentieth century, Ottawa set up CBC Radio, then TV, then satellite networks with a mandate to provide equal access in all regions.

Today, Canada prides itself on being a multicultural nation, even using this ideology on the international stage to foster prestige and encourage trade, investment and business immigration. Yet, our media system has a long way to go to reflect the real diversity of the population. In terms of regional variation, Canada's media system has slipped badly thanks to the ongoing cuts to CBC local news and public affairs. Diversity seems like a low priority in the leading newspapers, especially the *Globe and Mail*, which talks mainly to the cultural and political elites. The *Toronto Star* and *Winnipeg*

Free Press do a better job at reflecting the concerns of a broader public, although not to the extent that challenges the basic tenets of Canadian capitalism.

True diversity would entail a broad range of editorial opinion and a fundamental change to hiring practices in the dominant media. Our journalism and communications schools are filled with the full range of young Canadians — first or second generation students from Asia, Africa, Eastern Europe, South America and the Caribbean, as well as more women and First Nations students than ever, but this diversity is not reflected in the news rooms.

A major study in 2005 of Canadian news directors, the people who make key decisions in television news, concluded that "women and ethnic minorities are dramatically underrepresented in senior positions." The study also found that "the average news director is a white male who is well educated and comfortably middle-class."[1]

The authors of another wide-ranging study found that "local newscasts were dominated by stories about white people who saw the world through a prism of whiteness. These programs reinforced the construct of whiteness as the normative universe, a society in which essentially 'all others,' including people of colour — and especially Blacks and indigenous peoples — are constructed as 'problem' people."[2] Veteran broadcaster Rita Deverell says, "The CBC's own statistics tell us that as of 2006, people with disabilities in the CBC are 2.1 percent of the workforce. That's in any capacity. And members of visible minorities in any capacity are 5.7 percent of the workforce."[3]

Diversity would also include a broader range of opinion in current-affairs shows that feature guest panels of experts and interested parties. Even lifestyle programs fail to reflect our demographic reality. Too often on TV and radio racial minorities are either non-existent or lone standard bearers for their group. Too often racial minorities are discussed only in terms of problems facing their communities. Too often news and documentary programs use terms such as "mainstreet opinion" and "the heartland" as a shorthand for white people, implying that these folks are the real Canadians, the ones with a solid stake in our society, the backbone of the country.

The greatest gap in diversity centres on the role of Quebec in relation to the whole. Ignorance of each other's society and culture, the infamous two solitudes, surely represents a great squandering of opportunities to expand, enrich and improve the country as a whole. In the 1960s, the federal government set up programs to encourage student exchanges between English- and French-speakers, and thousands of young people jumped at the opportunity. Such schemes, as modest as they were, later slipped into oblivion, along with strong incentives for language translation. Quebec's filmmakers, artists, songwriters and TV producers are better known in Paris than in Toronto and Vancouver. Only in the 1970s, after the rise of an international film culture — of Truffaut, Bergman, Kurosawa and multiple new waves — did Quebec cinema gain traction in English Canada. Films such as *Mon oncle Antoine* and *Kamouraska*, which focused on the old rural Quebec, gained their deserved recognition. These were brilliant, complex films, and their long-lived reputations lie partly in the quality of the art and the depiction of human struggles. But other works, more modern, sour or politically challenging didn't sit so easily, at least on TV screens or in commercial theatres.

Film festivals have made great efforts at increasing visibility but commercial TV and theatre screens have no taste for Quebec whatsoever. In the view of John Ralston Saul, English-Canadian intellectuals have much to answer for in this situation, as few have bothered to become bilingual. Too many books on culture, politics and social issues ignore Quebec entirely, using the excuse that Quebec is too difficult or too foreign and therefore not necessary or appropriate to include. How many authors even try to familiarize themselves with Quebec culture let alone attempt an understanding? Unfortunately, I too have been guilty of this and it is my loss. So, at the risk of generalizing, I attempt to speak of Quebec in this book.

Diversity then is a key topic of conversation in Canada. In Toronto, difference from the U.S.; in Quebec, difference from les

Anglais; and among many, many ethnic and racial groups, difference from the White Man. This is only proper. But diversity should be embraced as a strength. The knowledge of diversity, combined with ideas of what brings us together, our points of commonality, takes that one step further. And that combination appeals greatly to most working people. Unfortunately, it is rarely practised in our dominant media.

Nationalism

Most Canadians do not partake of extreme nationalism. They're fine with the double life of living in Canada yet surrounded by U.S. culture. Contradictions are okay. Most feel proud or lucky that they were born or have immigrated here. But the government and big elites often have specific purposes for nationalism. They use it to overrun and integrate the West and the East, to keep the aspirations of Quebec in check, to hold off the pull of the U.S. and most recently to construct what they call the "Canadian Brand," a business image to send to the world. Thus, Canadian nationalism is also an ideology created to justify imperial, racist and commercial goals.

Some cultural critics have proposed broad theories suggesting that the huge scale of Canada, its harsh climate and small population have shaped our means of communication. One influential idea is that the scale of the country led the federal government to emphasize communications as a key element in nation-building. Consequently, the development of nationalist themes in media became the highest priority for the business and intellectual elites. The size of the country also may explain why Canada took an early lead in satellite broadcasting and the development of the internet.

As for the harsh climate, some writers maintain that Canadian media have until recently placed undo emphasis on rural and non-urban themes. This has often conflicted with Canada's international goals, at times on the lookout for more immigrants and at other times striving for more trade and investment. Focusing on our harsh climate doesn't encourage either of these goals. "No snow scenes," said an immigration bureaucrat to CPR filmmakers in the 1890s.

A nation is usually defined as a people united by language, ethnicity, culture, institutions and a shared heritage. When all or most of those elements are in place we usually see that a nation state has been constructed as well. In Canada, we have some of those elements and a strong state; Quebec has what many believe is a nation, but no state. During the past thirty years, the dominant ideas about nationalism in both English Canada and Quebec have been profoundly shaken by significant immigration of new ethnic and racial groups and by the growing power of many First Nations. Canada, says Mary Vipond, "is not an easy country to define, to govern or to imagine."[4]

Leftist critics of the dominant uses of nationalism have debated the "national question" since the 1880s. Is it necessary for Canada to become completely independent from Britain and the U.S. before creating a more equal society? Or is nationalism simply the ideology of the Canadian elite created to divert working people from more important goals? Does anti-Americanism merely displace the need for anti-capitalist battles? Will Canadian capitalists behave any differently when they become dominant? Since the 1960s, most progressive Canadians have linked nationalist goals with a more just society. Fewer and fewer people see any benefit in connecting too closely with the massive problems churning within the U.S. The challenge for the left today in terms of media is to convince Canadians that political independence does not mean that our economic system differs greatly from other capitalist countries. In fact, the hyper-globalization of today makes it even more difficult to create media structures outside the dominant forms.

Canadian nationalist culture has its conservative and its populist promoters. Beginning in the television-era of the 1950s, traditional conservatives have believed in Canadian culture because, compared to the U.S. fare, it stands for quality and more traditional values. It is less flashy, less attracted to sex and violence, less addicted to celebrities. It stands out for its serious drama, educational documentaries, non-commercial radio, gentle comedy, etc.

Canada's left-wing populists say that Canadian stories about ordinary folks are more enjoyable and useful because we see reflections of ourselves and our neighbours. We share geography, history and work experience, so these programs mean more to us. They help create our identity. The populists, however, must deal with a profound irony. Our popular culture is not particularly Canadian; it beams, trucks and flows from south of the border. Often, Canadian culture seems like the opposite of a popular culture, which, by definition, should be enjoyed by the majority of working people. It's true that many citizens live happily in a Canadian cultural universe, with genuine enjoyment and preference for *Corner Gas* and *Bon Cop Bad Cop*, K'naan and Sarah McLachlan, *Trailer Park Boys* and CBC Radio and. But these people are still a minority.

The media landscape of Quebec has always caused uneasiness among federalists because it often emphasizes the difficulties of living under "English" rule. In addition, the role of Catholicism in much of Quebec culture seems anathema to a society schooled in the progress of the Protestantism. For many, Quebec culture stands for an anachronistic past of rural and family values, while Canada as a whole is striving for a new industrial, individualist society.

Nationalism is thus the second great issue running through Canadian media since the nineteenth century. Federalist politicians were clear about how Canadian culture could be used to forge a unified country, perhaps uneasily including Quebec. From the academic painters of the late nineteenth century, to the founders of national museums, to the bureaucrats behind the CBC and the NFB, to the visionaries of the Massey Commission in 1952, who set up the Canada Council, Canadian unity was the stated goal. True, this mission meant independence from stifling Britain and the steamroller of commercial culture from the South, but it was also explicitly designed to suppress the aspirations of Quebec politicians. At best, even when tolerated, Quebec's artists, with their different experiences and concerns, just didn't fit the program. Marc Raboy, a leading media historian, argues that the federal government began to abandon the CBC in the 1980s when it became clear that the costs of maintaining the corporation no longer outweighed its benefits as an effective promoter of nationalism, especially national unity.[5]

Nationalism in Canada also works in tandem with anti-Americanism, from the huckster Sam Slick, of Slickville, in Thomas Haliburton's novels of the 1830s, to the comics of the 1950s, to the crassness of today's *American Idol*. For some, the principal reality is that we're not Americans. This resistance to the U.S. runs through most sectors of the arts and politics and even includes artists and media people otherwise quite hostile to a strong state in general.

The U.S. media industries still dominate the world — an $11 billion per year business just for commercial films distributed in the U.S. and Canada.[6] This vast sum translates into millions of jobs in several regions plus activity in hundreds of supporting businesses — hospitality, tourism, services, paper, technology and advertising. Indeed, the U.S. media sector is the only part of the economy that maintains a trade surplus; in these days, when the U.S. trade deficit runs into the trillions of dollars, such a sector is highly valued.

In addition to the domestic economic success story, the U.S. entertainment media have always worked closely with the country's State Department to ensure international markets and favourable trade laws. In return, the quality and glamour of U.S. films, TV and music have provided an appealing public face to U.S. governments for a hundred years, often playing the leading role in legitimizing the U.S. state around the world. Those media forms symbolize the American Way. Even in France, where governments have struggled to hold back the U.S. cultural tide, millions of French citizens flock to Hollywood movies every week. Inside the theatre, they are treated to some of the most talented artists and actors in the world, performing in the most expensive media products ever devised. Audiences usually come away with a favourable opinion of the U.S., still a land of endless possibilities.

Cultural Cringe or Canuxploitation

Some films are so bad that most Canadians would banish them from any association with national culture. Most of these fit into one or more of the genres scorned by mainstream critics, such as horror, cheap sci-fi, sex comedies and soft porn. We might assume that such fare serves primarily as exercises in the conventions of genres. Perhaps then they might stand a chance with an international audience; in other words they would show no connection with the specifics of Canadiana. But many of these films contain plenty of Canadian content, included as serious elements or tossed off as an in-joke or simply there in the background, barely noticed by filmmakers or audience. In the following list, the names of the actors and directors have been omitted as a gesture of kindness:

Apres-Ski (1971); *Diary of a Sinner* (1974); *Born for Hell,* aka *Naked Massacre* (1976); *Starship Invasions* (1977); *Overdrawn at the Memory Bank* (1983) "Without exaggeration, the absolute worst production values of any Canuxploitation film"; *Flesh Gordon Meets the Cosmic Teenagers* (1989).

Source: Paul Corupe, *Canuxploitation: Your Complete Guide to the Canadian B-Film* <www.caunuxploitation. com>.

Nationalism in broadcasting brought us the gentle comedy of *Jake and the Kid* and *Les Plouffes* in the 1950s, *Degrassi* in the 1980s, *Black Harbour,* from Nova Scotia, in the 1990s and more recently *Slings and Arrows,* from Stratford, Ontario, and *Republic of Doyle,* from Newfoundland. These well-made, timely series reflect specific regions of the country and travel well for export. Unfortunately, hundreds of other programs raked in federal support but were no different than their B-grade U.S. cousins. These are best forgotten.

Few nationalists in the film and TV business would argue that federal officials should dictate the specifics of Canadian content or that the industry should produce stories set exclusively in Canada. In fact, countless media people claim that they are working on a two-stage strategy, in which the industry first builds its technical

For and Against Cultural Nationalism	
PRO	CON
Our values are different, we need to have that reflected	American shows are just better — we should let the market decide
U.S. dominance is a habit based primarily on advertising	Canadian culture really just reflects the tastes of elites in Ontario and Quebec
We need the government to support and protect Canadian culture	We should be thinking about global culture and not cut ourselves off by favouring Canadian content
We believe in universal access for basic communications and media	The private sector always provides services more cheaply and more efficiently

skills and develops infrastructure, which will then form the base on which truly Canadian material can be produced. First we gain skills by working under the Americans, then we graduate to stand on our own. What irony then that the most financially successful Canadian film ever is *Porky's* (Bob Clark, 1981), a teen-boys gross-out hit, set in Florida. As of 2010 it had raked in $111 million at the box office. Would the depiction of young folks in Medicine Hat have produced something different? Perhaps so.

The ideology of cultural nationalism also supports a significant economic sector. Film, TV, radio, internet and advertising make up a sizeable industry, which means jobs — about 131,000 in 2009. Consequently, it's an industry that needs Canadian stories and government support.

The United States remains the most powerful country in the world, and as its neighbour, Canada has always been aware of that. The U.S. has ten times the population, a formidable state structure, powerful corporations and vast talents in all the artistic, scientific, and business fields. It also maintains the largest, most aggressive military, a force that sustains the U.S. economy as the major consumer of manufactured goods. It would be a mistake, however, to think that the U.S. has attained international dominance entirely by force, size or wealth. It has also produced cultural goods of amazing creativity and value that are admired around the world. From Charlie Chaplin to Louis Armstrong, from *The Simpsons* to great actors such as Laura Linney and Denzel Washington, audiences legitimately love and admire U.S. culture, both in its minority and popular forms, from jazz to hip hop. This has made it difficult for a small country like Canada to compete.

Despite many attempts to offset the power of U.S. media, Canada is swamped by U.S. culture and opinions, delivered in ever more efficient ways into theatres, over the air, through cables and via satellite. The onslaught of the internet during the past fifteen years only adds to this cross-border flow. These new methods of distribution defy national borders, making it almost impossible to lessen the tide.

Over the last four decades Hollywood films have staked out 95 percent of the screens in Canadian theatres. This is so taken for granted that U.S. film distributors refer to Canada as a domestic market, more or less identical to the U.S. Even with strict Canadian content rules, radio also remains dominated by U.S. artists. And in TV, the most popular medium, U.S. shows make up the vast majority for drama, comedy and sports. Even the CBC dips into the southern ocean when it needs a sure-fire money maker, although in some cases the negative publicity of showing something like *American Idol* or *Wheel of Fortune* creates more trouble than benefits.

The average Hollywood feature film now requires an $80 million budget. In Canada the average budget is $3 million. This has both positive and negative effects. On the one hand, it forces Canadian artists to do more with less; competition leads them to aim for U.S. quality even when their budgets are paltry, and often they succeed. On the other hand, the U.S. model of lavish budgets encourages a blockbuster mentality in Canada, so that fewer productions get more money. Diversity and experiment receive short shrift. Remarkably, many film and TV producers have been able to create a different sort of storytelling unique to Canada and Quebec, especially those who flaunt Canadian popular culture and don't try to imitate too closely the U.S. genres. *SCTV*, Bob and Doug McKenzie, *Les Plouffes*, *Trailer Park Boys*, *Corner Gas* and *Cruising Bar* all work within mainstream genres but certainly don't hide their Canadian-ness.

Within the music business, Canadians have fared well, with a significant number staying in Canada, thereby creating a vibrant music culture that is both inventive and genuinely popular. Of course, Canadians boast when a local makes it in the U.S. — although it's best when such stars remember their roots and return here every so often — Canadian music fans seem a tolerant lot. Hank Snow, Joni Mitchell, Oscar Peterson and Diana Kroll stand out because they do well internationally but keep a big toe at home. But just as many Canadians seem to get sucked into the most commercial genres of Nashville and Los Angeles — a continual drain of talent away from Canadian popular culture.

The newspaper industry seems like the sector least affected by the U.S. Regulations within Canada's Income Tax Act ensure that newspaper ownership remains in Canadian hands. However Canadian papers apparently feel that they must follow the general trends in U.S. magazines, TV and films toward a celebrity culture. Running a story on a B-grade American actor or the Academy Awards sells Canadian newspapers and also allows for cheaper journalism.

Canadian papers rely on U.S. popular culture to reach a younger audience or maintain their hipness. Higher brow columnists look to the *New York Times* and *The New Yorker* for ideas and trend spotting (some of which get credited). With the popularity of online news reading of such papers as the *Onion*, *Slate* and *Huffington Post*, especially by younger folks, this blend of U.S. and Canadian cultural references has become more prevalent. And Canadian newspapers can't rely on a foreign newspaper blackout as in the old days. On the other hand, with a few exceptions, the U.S. newspaper product, such as *USA Today*, is so inferior and devoid of news that there may be little to worry about.

Since the passing of the North American Free Trade Agreement (NAFTA) in 1994, many nationalists have worried that Canada's media legislation and rules on foreign ownership will be eroded. For example, Canadian newspapers and book publishers must be, by law, primarily Canadian owned. This form of protection could be challenged by U.S. companies or their government. While Canada has the right to some types of protection for its media, the U.S. may retaliate in another sector of the economy. A new Canadian law in film distribution, for example, could be countered with new U.S. tariffs on lumber.

The State

The state needs the media to communicate its policies, deliver its ideology, promote its agenda on a world stage and provide an educated workforce with the information it and its employers need. For these reasons, the Canadian government will never allow free enterprise competition or a monopoly to decimate any media sector or allow a foreign takeover. Canadian newspapers may be in trouble with their business model resulting in lower profits than in the past, but the government will undoubtedly step in if foreign companies try to take over or if a major paper folds because its shareholders abandon it. The same holds for book publishing.

The "State or the States" remains the ongoing question for the cultural industries. How can we use the resources of the federal government to make programs or profits we want to see, rather than being swamped by American companies. Independent filmmakers often reluctantly accept the strings of the CBC or NFB in order to complete their work. Commercial cable and TV broadcasters lobby for more protection from foreign interests, even as they buy more cut-rate American products. For example, the private TV networks CTV

Communications Media and Nation-Building

1852 — Electric Telegraph Act, Province of Canada
1890s — Bell Canada dominates telephone communications
1936 — Creation of CBC Radio
1952 — CBC Television goes on-air
1939 — Creation of the National Film Board of Canada
1970s — Bailout and subsidies to Canadian book publishers
1960s and 1970s — Canadian content rules for TV and radio
1932, 1958, 1991 — Broadcasting Acts
1993 — Telecommunications Act
1972 — Launch of Canada's Anik A-I communications satellite
1990s — Major funding for internet networks
1995 — Federal government advertising campaign targets Quebec, resulting in the Sponsorship Scandal
2006 — Senate report expresses concern over media concentration (as in royal commissions in 1971 and 1981.)

and Global rail on at the unfair advantages of the "state-supported" CBC but profit handsomely from their monopoly of lucrative U.S. TV, made possible by the Broadcasting Act, which excludes foreign competition. Book retailer Chapters Indigo, which controls more than 70 percent of bookstore sales in Canada, also holds this monopoly position thanks to the federal foreign ownership restrictions, which keep out U.S. giants such as Barnes and Noble.

Beginning in the nineteenth century, Canadians have created entertainment and distributed news that matters to its citizens. And Canadian governments have experimented with all manner of laws, incentives and subsidies to create or protect Canadian-specific communications. Many of these initiatives have walked hand-in-hand with nation-building itself. Canada's federal government has played a major role in the development of media systems since Confederation. In addition to setting up the CBC/Radio Canada for radio and TV, and the NFB/ONF for film, the government and its agencies have tried many other methods to create, support and protect our communications media. These projects were based on the example of the inter-continental telegraph and rail lines, in the 1880s.

Some of these government initiatives are well-known and visible, such as direct grants to publishers and TV producers; other important forms of support are less obvious. Most other Western governments use these practices as well, although trade disputes often flare up in this era when we're all supposedly free traders. From the 1950s to the 1990s, the government provided postal subsidies for delivering books and magazines. At different times a quota system attempted to get Canadian music and films air or screen time. Radio stations must now program 35 percent Canadian music each day: that scheme has been tremendously successful. A quota for films, however, failed miserably.

Since the creation of the various federal media programs, starting with the Canada Council in the 1950s, the Department of Culture's book publishing subsidies of the 1970s, and moving through Telefilm Canada and the Broadcasting and Telecommunications Acts of the 1980s, news and entertainment media in Canada have looked to the federal government for support. Without that support, everyone would be working for the Americans and probably not telling Canadian stories or reporting Canadian news.

Creators and producers often receive tax breaks by hiring Canadian artists and technicians. Other legislation has targeted ownership issues, ensuring that foreigners do not acquire controlling interest in essential communication media, such as book publishing, film production and newspapers. Still other programs have supported international distribution and travel to festivals and trade shows. This is not a case of state versus private interests but rather an attempt to keep Canadian media in the hands of Canadian capitalists. In addition, Canada, like most governments, including the U.S., supports its cultural industries through technical training programs and specialized media arts education. Municipal governments also assist by making locations available for filming and providing police security, road closures, management expertise, etc. Well-healed productions are the focus of considerable competition between cities, provinces and U.S. states, and most major cities have created special agencies to lure such business.

On balance, Canada has created a mixed economy in which the most cut-throat forms of capitalism are modulated and tamped down by the federal government and its agencies. But the mix is not equal because the imperatives of capitalist competition and profit-taking set the context for everyone, even those media with state support. As mentioned above, even the CBC must compete aggressively for advertising. Although the NFB has achieved some independence, its films have never found reliable exhibition in commercial theatres or on television.

What is often overlooked is that the federal government plays the role of a facilitator for private interests. In the past thirty years, it has paid for cable TV, satellite and computer infrastructures, which were then handed over to media corporations. Although the CBC clearly benefited as well, without the federal government, private broadcast media in Canada would barely exist. To the extent that modern newspapers rely on digital production, distribution and now journalism itself, they have benefited as well.

The federal government's use of the media, especially advertising, precipitated the biggest scandal of the 1990s. Following the 1995 referendum in Quebec, in which the sovereignty forces lost by only a slim margin, Jean Chrétien's government poured millions into ads in Quebec that primarily promoted federal projects and cultural initiatives. It also used money to reward Liberal-friendly advertising executives and owners. Many deals were awarded without proper bidding or even formal contracts. In the end, the province was blanketed in federal propaganda, several executives went to jail, many politicians lost their seats and the government changed hands.

Capitalism

This morning at breakfast I'm greeted with ecstatic headlines in *The Globe and Mail*: "Private sector fuels stunning surge in jobs"; "Near record hiring in June…, restoring most recession losses…"; "The handoff from public to private spending looks to be going smoothly." I remember all those folks who lost their jobs in the past two years, following the bank crisis in the U.S. I recall all those small businesses down the street that simply disappeared, to be replaced with "For Lease" signs. But when I think back to the last "recession," not that long ago, I remember that most of those lost and regained jobs shifted from full-time to part-time. People who'd had good manufacturing salaries ended up in low-paid service work. Seventeen paragraphs along in *The Globe*'s story, nearly buried at the end comes this important fact: "Another concern is the type of jobs being created. Retail and other service-sector jobs tend to be more temporary, based on flexible hours, and are often lower-paying."

Here is the ideology of capitalism at work. Thousands of workers lose their jobs, and some get back crummy alternatives. Their new work hours take on a pleasant-sounding ring — "flexible." The private sector shows its strength and takes over again from government spending. Who decided that this front-page story would be defined as "stunning?" Who stuck in the current cliché of "surge," first used by the U.S. military in Iraq? Who decided that we should be lucky to compare ourselves to the Americans with their higher rate of unemployment? This framing of the issues and use of language suggests that the economic system is humming along as it should. The free market and the private sector have done their job. Too bad about the loss of those good jobs, but after all "There is no alternative."

Capitalism is the basis on which our entire economy works and, for many, the explanation for why it works so well. Yet most history textbooks and films simply take this for granted or make no mention of it. We get the history of liberalism and parliamentary democracy, the development of a factory system and the growth of cities, but almost nothing on the economic system. The same sleight-of-hand prevails on TV. As we have seen, the CBC's lavish documentary series, *Canada, A People's History*, promoted itself as history from the bottom up, that is, history focusing on ordinary Canadians, thereby ignoring larger economic debates.

Like every other in North America and Western Europe, Canadian media work primarily to legitimate this country's political and corporate elites and capitalism in general. Most of the time Canadian newspapers and TV comprise a set of dominant institutions that push other voices and points of view to the margins. Journalists within the system and citizens on the outside sometimes manage to introduce countervailing ideas, but this requires an uphill battle.

We can also compare Canada's media to that of the U.S, Britain and France. In some respects Canada's record is stronger; in other areas it falls well short. Canada's form of capitalism differs from that of Britain and the U.S., yet it shares many of the same characteristics. The country is founded on the belief that the pursuit of profit and the mechanisms of competition will lead to the best standard of living for all. Through this system Canadians will have jobs and the best quality, lowest-priced goods. Market competition drives poor companies out and rewards those who make goods that people want to buy, at a reasonable price. Unlike the U.S., Canada's economic development has always favoured large corporate entities that operate in positions of monopoly or oligopoly. This has required a more active state, which plays the role of regulator. In the realm of communications, the railways and telephone services provided the standard models. In more recent times, the federal government has played a major role in funding and regulating cable, computing and satellite infrastructures. In the U.S. these infrastructures have been influenced more directly through corporate or military activity, facilitated by the state.

The creation of the CBC, for radio in the 1930s, then TV in the 1950s, cut against the grain of the free market. Thus, they were greeted with open hostility by private interests who had hoped Canada would follow the U.S. path. These private media companies and their right-wing backers continue their campaign today against the CBC. While Canada's ruling groups don't always see eye-to-eye or share identical interests, these conflicts aren't as clear cut as government versus big business.

Media For Profit

The state plays a big role in regulating the mediascape and directly subsidizes the CBC and TV and film production. Nevertheless, dominant roles are shared by private broadcasters and production companies, who operate for profit and answer to shareholders. In this climate, CBC TV competes for advertising and must compare its ratings and viewer numbers with those of CTV and Global. In addition, it must also bid for U.S. programs.

The corporate media model, which requires the highest rate of profit, affects both news and entertainment programs in several ways. Sometimes owners decide that creating a better product will attract advertisers or subscribers, and they spend more to make it happen. Usually, however, this represents a long-term strategy and owners or their shareholders don't wish to wait, preferring to see their profits this year. The only other way to improve profits is to cut costs. For newspapers and broadcasters there are several ways to do this:

- cut editorial and journalist salaries;
- emphasize short-term stories, within specific popular genres;
- bow to pressure from advertisers or influential persons to cover or avoid certain stories;
- produce material that appeals to the broadest or most lucrative "demographic";
- produce lifestyle segments and programs that serve the interests of advertisers;
- avoid structural problems in the economy, replaced by micro-economics, management, marketing and business success;

- emphasize the ups and downs of the stock markets accompanied by almost complete avoidance of labour issues; and
- produce TV and films that work well for export, to the U.S. and elsewhere, thus favour U.S. styles, subjects and genres (*CSI*, *The Border*, etc.)

Corporate trends have driven all but the biggest out of the market, so that CTV, Global and Irving play dominant roles, and corporate laws allow companies to sue critics due to supposed harm to trademarks or hindrance of trade. In British Columbia, CanWest newspapers sued several artists in 2009, who created and distributed a satiric front page of the *Vancouver Sun*. The critique focused on the stridently pro-Israel slant of CanWest papers. CanWest argued that the satire damaged their brand or trademark. Ignoring the issues of free speech, they instead framed the challenge in economic terms. Within the newspaper world, the role of competition is much clearer due to fewer direct subsidies and little regulation of content (TV news must show balance, whereas newspapers are free to editorialize or take political sides). Newspapers often enter into price wars and show a long-term trend of cutting serious journalism. Most recently, Canadian newspapers have started "outsourcing" many of their tasks, including accounting, printing, advertising and even copy-editing. For example, in 2008, the CanWest newspaper chain outsourced its advertising work to a company based in India and The Philippines.

As has been the ironic trend for many years in Canada and elsewhere, unchecked competition eventually leads to oligopoly or monopoly. While theoretically, new entrepreneurs are free to jump in, the cost of entry prevents all but the very biggest and richest from joining the fray.

Underneath these general trends toward cost-cutting, maintaining profits and the long slide in quality, a broad corporate agenda shapes our entire media system. Consider the case of the 1992 Westray mining disaster, in Plymouth, Nova Scotia, in which twenty-six miners were killed. A thorough media study afterwards found that from a sample of 365 articles on Westray, written over two months, only one dealt with safety from a worker's perspective.[7] More generally, all of the coverage failed to consider Westray to be a corporate crime. It was mostly portrayed as a techno-disaster, with some bad apple managers complicating the tragedy.

In the reporting on environmental issues, especially those that directly affect Canadian business, a corporate agenda lurks behind most of the coverage. Robert Babe of the University of Western Ontario studied the *Globe and Mail* coverage of the Kyoto accords, in which Canada agreed to cut its emissions of greenhouse gases. Babe found that the paper treated the issue as a business and economics story, or a story of Ottawa politics. Babe looked at hundreds of headlines, columns, news items, editorials, etc. and found that the great bulk of the *Globe*'s Kyoto coverage was negative. He also found many inaccuracies and a tendency to treat industry statements as fact.[8]

James Winter at the University of Windsor has researched many similar examples of corporate points of view shaping media coverage. These beliefs about the economic system are so pervasive that they now seem natural. Winter summarizes some of the "lies the media tell us":

- "That which governs least, governs best. The unfettered free market system is the fairest and best guiding principle."
- "Public ownership such as crown corporations [such as the post office] are wasteful and inefficient, serving no real useful purpose."
- "Democracy and capitalism are synonymous and interchangeable. You can't have one without the other."[9]

Advertising

In our system of corporate media, advertising greases most of the wheels. Companies make their money through selling ads, much more than through subscriptions or single sales. Of course, having many viewers, listeners, surfers and readers is still important because it shows advertisers where their target market spends its time. In fact, advertising works as an active factor in "managing demand" for products. There are classified ads, display ads for businesses, large and small, government ads and public relations-type ads placed by governments, industry and lobby groups. The media historian Paul Rutherford bluntly calls this latter type of advertising propaganda. It's a "persistent and ubiquitous barrage" that masquerades as public service, public relations and social marketing, says Rutherford. Examples include anti-drug and stop smoking campaigns, pronuclear, pro-tar sands and asbestos industry campaigns, Canada Day celebrations and provincial business and tourism promotions.[10]

The creating, buying and selling of advertising is a major business in itself, generating $6.6 billion in 2008. Some of the country's most talented artists get drawn into advertising, as do actors, computer experts, sociologists, cinematographers, editors and writers. Even Canada's best film and TV directors work at least part-time in advertising. Moreover, many observers of contemporary culture believe that advertising now provides the primary discourse for images and storytelling. Whether that's true or not, advertising often sets the tone for appropriate behaviour and mores. It also sets the frame of the sovereign individual and leads us to believe that through consumption we create ourselves — an individual to present to the world.

Concentration and Convergence

The trend for media companies in the West has been toward concentration, or fewer companies and owners, and more recently toward convergence, or owners who operate in several different types of media. With concentration, we get the rise of newspaper chains controlled by one group or family. With convergence we get the same owners controlling newspapers, radio stations, TV broadcasts and internet distribution. Convergence means that some owners carry out two tasks: they create content *and* control its distribution.

> ## Growing the Company
>
> Horizontal — concentration, for example, one newspaper buys another.
> Vertical — concentration, for example, a cable company buys a TV production company.
> Diagonal — convergence, for example, a telephone company buys a TV network.

From the 1970s onward, Canadian newspaper chains grew larger and larger and attracted the attention of several government reports and commissions, which worried about the trend. But the buzzword of the new century was convergence, creating even more worry about the influence of Quebecor or BCE, which control companies in all media sectors.

In 1981, Tom Kent, a former newspaper executive, chaired a famous royal commission on newspapers. Twenty years later he still believed that "concentration has narrowed the range and lowered the quality of information… readily available. Everywhere, from St. John's to Victoria, it has diminished press concern with local affairs…. For the country as a whole, it cramps the expression of diverse opinions."[11] Kent also states, somewhat ironically, that convergence is particularly dangerous because it means that newspapers come within the world of broadcasting licences, making them *less* independent from the government of the day. TV stations must get a licence and promise to be "balanced" in their political coverage, he says. Newspapers need no such licence and thus, in theory, have more independence from the government. TV stations make far more money than newspapers. "For BCE, the *Globe and Mail* [was] financially unimportant beside its stablemate, CTV."[12] Therefore, according to Kent, "Freedom of the press is compromised because the fortunes of its proprietors are determined chiefly by the TV licences for which they go, cap in hand, to government." This argument assumes too much that business and government want to be independent from each other, but in general it seems a valid concern.

Concentration of Newspapers

1970 — two chains owned 58 percent of Canada's newspapers (Southam and Thomson)

1980 — two chains owned 71 percent of Canada's newspapers (Southam and Thomson)

2010 — two chains own 60 percent of Canada's newspapers (Postmedia, formerly CanWest, and Quebecor)

The Shark Tank
All of these business groups are circling each other looking for a weak company to swallow.

Cable companies — BCE, Rogers, Shaw, Quebecor, etc.

Telephone companies — BCE, Telus, Rogers, etc.

Distributors — Quebecor, etc.

Producers — Corus, Astral, Alliance, etc.

Newspaper chains — Quebecor, Postmedia, Torstar, etc.

Broadcasters — CBC, Shaw, CTV, etc.

Investors — Onex, Goldman Sachs, etc.

See Appendix for company details.

New Brunswick holds the unfortunate honour of living with the most media concentration in the country. Professor Erin Steuter of UNB, who has studied the Irving media companies for many years, puts it this way: "Living in New Brunswick where all of the English language daily papers are owned by a single large capitalist enterprise means that the voice of the corporate world speaks loudly and the coverage of labour focuses on confrontational and controversial events such as strikes in which labour is scapegoated."[13] For example, Steuter observed that, during a major strike in 2003, "all three papers ran editorials… critical of the community college and prison custodians who were walking the picket line." She noted that terms such as irrational, unreasonable, ludicrous and greedy were "peppered throughout the editorials revealing a pattern of Irving coverage of labour issues that typically portrays labour as the active and disruptive party."

The commercial media have mastered the cover-up of economic

realities with claims that newspapers and broadcasting are in crisis because of lower advertising revenue and higher costs. Yet profits continue to climb, even after the 2008 recession. In June 2010, Shaw Communications reported a 20 percent increase in profits over the previous year. Rogers radio stations in Ontario posted 30 percent rates of profit in 2009, and Quebecor has raised $100 million to start its right-wing SunTV network.[14]

The Public

The Canadian public is a fabulously diverse group, characterized by myriad differences of region, class, ethnicity, race, language, religion, gender, etc. Any attempts to talk about "the public" in general terms will fail. That doesn't mean that Canadians of all kinds don't have lots in common. We all live by the standards of liberal democracy, driven by an economy of capitalism and organized by a central state. By world standards, Canadians are relatively well-off, healthy and educated. These common features get reflected in our media — both its structure and content — they give us the CRTC, which strives for universal service across the country, and they give us *Rookie Blue*, a generic, U.S.-style cop show that reflects our faith in police and our fear of "criminal elements." They give us media dominated by liberal individualism and consumption through advertising *and* at the same time a strong tradition of documentaries that highlight social problems.

While we can easily study how Canadian governments have tried to use the media, it is much more difficult to study Canadian audiences. Who are the people who watch Canadian TV dramas? Who reads newspapers and for what purpose? How do we use the various media forms to make sense in our lives? What impact does advertising have on our sense of self; what impact do political documentaries have on our sense of social responsibility? These questions concern the effects of media. How have the broadcasting media changed Canadian politics? Have the CBC and the private networks brought Canadians into the modern world — made them more alike — reflected regional differences? Unfortunately, Canadian scholars have not taken much interest in these questions, especially in how they might have been answered differently in the past.

One group that has consistently asked some of these questions is the advertisers. To do this they hand the job to private companies such as the Bureau of Broadcast Measurement (BBM) and the Nielsen Company. For example, a newspaper or TV station can use the BBM statistics to see the age and income of those interested in particular topics or programs. Media executives are most concerned with those groups with the most money to spend — so we know the most about young men in their twenties and well-off urban dwellers. One reason for corporate excitement about the internet is its ability to track and measure the interests and habits of Canadians, the better to target advertising.

We need to remember that when talking about Canadian governments or the Canadian state in general we are not always talking about the public. In a democratic society we hope that those who run the government represent the needs and wishes of the public, but sadly, that is rarely the case. What is good for the state is not of the same value to various publics.

There are two ways of talking about the Canadian public: in terms of social class and in terms of civil society. As for class, as Karl Marx and many others have argued since, all capitalist societies are divided primarily into a working class and a ruling class. The ruling class, which is a small minority of people, not only has more money but controls the corporations, the state and the dominant ideologies. The working class is comprised of the vast majority, who don't have the means to control industry or the ruling ideas. In Canada, as elsewhere, however, working people have the ability to form organizations and exert their power. They also have the ability to resist dominant ideologies and replace them with sets of ideas more appropriate to their lives. However, the concentration of media in corporate control limits the ability of the working class to communicate and organize. Using the lens of class analysis, the Canadian public is its working class — a group very different from the state and the corporations. We might also compare the reality of working people's lives with how they are depicted in our news and entertainment media. Which gets more attention, for example, the stock market or deaths and injuries on the job; the business models of corporations or layoffs and declining wages?

Looking at Canada in terms of civil society, we see things a little differently. Civil society, or the public sphere as it's sometimes called, refers to all those groups, organizations and activities that occupy a place outside the realms of the state and corporations. So, the churches, environmental groups, unions, women's, neighbourhood and anti-racism organizations all form part of civil society. That doesn't mean that they have no interaction with the state or corporations, but usually their allegiance remains somewhat separate. In this model of society, working-class people may end up participating with those we might define as poor and of the middle-class. Indeed, these sorts of ad-hoc or strategic alliances are common in Western societies. That doesn't mean that people engaged in civil society activities reject a social class analysis, but they often feel that their lives can be defined and shaped by many different factors.

Many writers have looked at civil society as the means for moving beyond corporate and state agendas. This explains the excitement in many quarters about social media and the rise of citizen journalists — these may be the forums in which groups within civil society can make their voices heard. Both these approaches to the public remind us that the state and the public are not identical.

During the battle to establish a non-commercial national radio network in Canada during the 1930s, this distinction between public media and state media became apparent. Marc Raboy explains in his essential book *Missed Opportunities*:

> The story of Canadian broadcasting illustrates the need to distinguish "national" from "public" interests — and that

the tendency to confuse the two ends up turning broadcasting into an instrument of state policy with all that this
implies. Thus broadcasting policy in Canada has been
made to serve the broader political agenda of the state as its
priorities change from time to time — one day the need for
national unity in the face of perceived threats of external or
internal adversity, the next day the promotion of economic
development of local capitalist industry, the following day
dealing with the social pressures and demands for a more
equitable distribution of wealth and resources.[15]

In the years before the CBC came into being, many well-organ-
ized groups fought for non-commercial, public broadcasting, that
is, broadcasting for the social good of its citizens not necessarily
the state, and certainly not simply for profits. In the U.S. the Public
Broadcasting Corporation has kept its name precisely in order to distinguish it from the hand of government, a hand that most Americans
viscerally fear in media. Canadians have never had such an aversion
to the state's role in their lives, even when it came to issues of speech
and expression, but in the 1930s, many groups were able to keep
the concepts of public and state quite separate. There is still debate
about whether the CBC has been able to keep that balance. There
are many public radio stations in Canada, based in universities and
community organizations. And in some areas of Canada's North,
First Nations radio certainly operates in the public realm.

Individual members of the public have a variety of interests,
experiences and needs. We don't just fit into one category. On any
given evening, I can listen to a political debate on radio, connect to
a popular music website, read a local paper and see a U.S. cop show.
Perhaps I'm a different "public" person in each case; perhaps I'm
confused about my "identity"; perhaps I'm just an average Canadian.
Beware, therefore, of people who talk in confident generalities about
the Canadian public.

The Conservative Party and the Canadian Media?

Conservatives, as was pointed out in Chapter One, share common complaints about the Canadian media system. But, naturally, not all groups think alike, and their opinions don't always jibe with those of Kory Teneycke. The following three strains of the conservative critique stand out.

A *populist and libertarian* critique bubbles up from those most offended by what they see as elitism and government meddling in citizens' lives. According to them, the Canadian media system is the product of bureaucrats from Ottawa and Toronto, completely out-of-touch with "ordinary" Canadians. This group wants access to more American programming because they see that as the most popular choice. As for Canadian news, they want less emphasis on Ottawa (i.e., Parliament) and more on "news you can use," which generally means more local fare. They classify CBC as "anti-mainstreet," meaning against the traditional values of white Canadians. For example, many feel that the CBC gives too much time to proponents of the federal gun registry, proving the broadcaster's urban bias. Outside of Quebec, this populist strain of conservatism often resents the amount of attention paid to Quebec in politics and in the media. These folks were also behind the anti-census rhetoric in 2010.

A segment of this group likes what they call "straight talk" of the kind that emanates from shock-jocks like Howard Stern in the U.S. and Jeff Fillion at CHOI in Quebec. When the CRTC yanked that station's licence in August 2004, because of Fillion's obscenity and hate speech, fifty buses holding 2,000 angry protesters descended on Parliament Hill.[16]

Another segment of this group, following the lead of the Harper government, criticizes the CBC for being "soft on crime" (not including people who defy the gun registry). Others feel that the CBC is often unpatriotic in its reporting on the war in Afghanistan. When leading right-wing commentators criticize the CRTC as a mechanism of "Government imposed cultural censorship" concerning music

---

"The Silencing of the Conservative Voice in Canada"

Here's how the traditionalist group Real Women sees the media:

- Most of the media, print, radio and TV in Canada, have no interest in providing balance in programming and reporting.
- There are only a handful of genuinely conservative journalists in Canada. Lorne Gunter of the *Edmonton Journal*, Claire Hoy, Ted Byfield, Licia Corbella (*Calgary Herald*), Susan Martinuk, Rory Leishman, David Warren and George Jonas of the *National Post*, come to mind. Others, such as the *National Post's* Andrew Coyne, although he places his toe in conservative waters, quickly withdraws it on such issues as same-sex marriage so as to indicate to his fellow (liberal) journalists, "See, I'm not all that unreasonable. 'I'm a moderate'!"
- The CRTC has consistently refused licences for religious broadcasting, with two exceptions. The CRTC granted a licence to a homosexual TV station (the first in the world), as well as to the Playboy channel. The CRTC acts as a censor by its federally appointed bureaucrats in determining Canadian "values." Obviously the CRTC does not believe that conservative values are "Canadian."

Source: Real Women, 2004 <http://realwomenca.com>.)

---

and TV Canadian content rules, they usually get enthusiastic support from this populist, libertarian sector of the right.[17] "Obviously the CBC felt it was essential to eliminate the third verse [to the 'Maple Leaf Forever'] as well," said Garry Toffoli, in the online magazine *Monarchist*, "as it was anathema to the media industry that exists by fostering animosity in Canada."[18]

A second conservative strain, which is basically *traditionalist*, voices a strong critique of Canada's media system but one that is much quieter than the loud and aggressive populists. Few of these people, such as Real Women, enjoy a regular platform in the mainstream media, and their numbers aren't what they used to be. Nonetheless, their views carry weight. These folks tend to be older and attached to the mainstream churches. They may also represent a growing sentiment among some older first-generation immigrant groups.

The Big Thinkers about Media

Harold Innis ranks as Canada's most important historian. His early work on the economy, known as the staples thesis, on the Canadian Pacific Railway, the fur trade and the cod fishery still provides the basis on which to understand how the country has developed. Late in his life, Innis switched his attention to communications and its economic and cultural significance. Although somewhat abstract, his concepts of how space and time shape communications, and how in turn these communications shape society, still carry great explanatory power. *The Bias of Communication*, written in 1951, outlines these theories.

Marshall McLuhan became an international celebrity in the 1960s by taking Innis's theories several steps further and applying them to radio, TV, print, advertising and globalization. His catchy phrase, "the global village" returned with a vengeance in the new century as a way of describing how connected we are to each other in the world. Another of his aphorisms, "the medium is the message" led him to discount the concepts of class power and to downplay the content within communications. But his belief that technologies (such as radio or computers) can profoundly shape what and how we communicate is an idea that must be given its due if we are to understand modern life. An entertaining, though not particularly critical introduction to McLuhan, is Kevin McMahon's film, *McLuhan's Wake* (2002).

Mary Vipond, of Concordia University in Montreal, comes nowhere near the fame of Innis or McLuhan. However, she has been writing about the Canadian media for thirty years. Her book *The Mass Media in Canada* is a standard text and her historical essays on the birth of the CBC, radio news and advertising have been influential. Although she rarely analyzes the class dynamics within Canadian media, she has educated many people about how the system works and how it came to be. In a 2009 summary she argues that the study of the media "has been hived off as a small, specialized sub-field." It must now expand, she says, to integrate women's history, many different approaches to culture and a global perspective. (See "Whence and Whither: The Historiography of Canadian Broadcasting" in Gene Allen ibid.)

The Radical Thinkers

Canadian writers who have provided a more radical approach to media have not yet produced broadly influential work to match Innis and McLuhan.

Dallas Smyth (1907–1992) and *Vincent Mosco* of Queen's University have written broad theories of the media which apply to Canada. Their work starts from a Marxist approach to society, emphasizing how the economy creates a class society and a state that upholds the power of owners and managers. Their political economy approach, which I use in this book, emphasizes how the combination of politics and economic factors shape our media.

Mosco warns of the new orthodoxy surrounding the internet. "Cyberspace gurus encourage us to think that we have reached the end of history, the end of geography and the end of politics. Everything has changed. So we can apply the mute button to whatever has come before. After all, history has nothing to say to us because it knows nothing of cyberspace.... We want to believe that our era is unique in transforming the world as we have known it. The end is preferred to more of the same; the transcendent to the routine; the sublime to the banal. So we not only view our age as revolutionary. We forget that others looked at earlier technologies in the same way." (Mosco, "From Here to Banality: Myths about New Media and Communication Policy," paper given at Carleton University, December 2002 <http://www.carleton.ca/ces/events/novemberconference2002/Mosco.pdf>.)

The work of Smyth and Mosco operates at a high level of technical language. This is important scholarship, but we also need works that will explain these ideas in a popular, accessible manner.

Marc Raboy is a Montreal-based scholar whose work goes furthest in using sophisticated theory written in a relatively accessible manner. While he has not yet provided an overview to match that of Mary Vipond, he has produced books and articles on many important subjects, especially *Missed Opportunities: The Story of Canada's Broadcasting Policy*. Raboy's distinction between public broadcasting and what he terms administrative broadcasting, of the state, is a key concept that I have applied in the book.

Within the traditionalist ranks, however, a much more aggressive Christian right-wing has made considerable headway since Stephen Harper took office. These people refer to the mainstream media as anti-Christian. Consequently, they have steadily been building their own media communications networks, such as the Christian Broadcasting Network, Crossroads, etc. on television, radio and the internet.[19]

Traditionalists believe that Canadian society has become atheist, too permissive and too negative, pointing to the film *Young People Fucking* (Martin Gero, 2008), from Quebec, as a clear example. Many believe that a fault lies with the Americanization of Canadian media, especially its crass, "excessively democratic" lack of values. These folks believe that the Canadian media actually hinders Canadian identity. They look at CBC programs such as *DaVinci's Inquest* and find it too negative, focusing only on the dregs of society in Vancouver. They also fault the CBC for dealing too often with social problems, for example, David Suzuki's *Nature of Things*, which many feel is overly critical of Canada. Unlike the populists, however, this group believes in the general mandate of the CBC as an exercise in nation-building and a bulwark against the heathens to the South.

The traditionalists obviously disagree with those populist conservatives who want more U.S. content and more uncensored talk radio. This disagreement within conservative ranks about the role of the U.S. and its popular culture runs right back to Confederation. These traditionalists really are conservative — they long for the old status quo.

Among Québécois, a similar strain of traditionalism looks back to the older days of a strong Catholic church and supposedly unified French-speaking communities. These sentiments even cross political lines between federalists and separatists. A film about the life and times of Rocket Richard is quite acceptable; a series such as *Les Boys* (Louis Saia, 1997), about a loutish group of tavern-dwellers, is not.

The third and most powerful strain of conservative thinking

emanates from the big media *business groups*. These include the private TV broadcasters, newspaper chains and large cable and telecommunications companies. Their views are vigourously communicated through right-wing groups such as the Fraser and C.D. Howe Institutes. Their general approach is to claim that they are just providing what Canadians want and that the government should not stand in the way. This is accompanied by more specific ideologies such as: The market should prevail. The CBC has an unfair advantage regarding advertising. The CBC is wasteful — we can do it better. The CRTC is meddlesome–it is anti-growth and anti-global. When it comes to such issues, there is little difference between English and French-language companies.

4. MEDIA IN QUEBEC

The modern period in Quebec, known as the Quiet Revolution (1960–1966), was ushered in by two major labour disputes. Both were bitter and symbolic. But these strikes were not in mining, the forests or manufacturing; they took place in the media. In 1958, the journalists and editors at North America's largest French-language newspaper, *La Presse*, went on strike. The following year a similar dispute involving TV and radio producers took place at Radio-Canada. The strikers attracted widespread sympathy because the fight was not just about work, it was about who would decide the future of Québécois culture. Would it be the media bosses or the creators and their audiences?

Most Canadians know that Quebec's history differs profoundly from that of the rest of Canada — the Ancien Regime, which was conquered by the English in 1759, the domination of the Catholic Church, the seigneury system of farming stretching like long fingers out from the St. Lawrence, French civil law. But most Canadians believe that all this is in the past. Surely, that stuffy old history has no bearing today. But they would be wrong. *Je me souviens* is not just a slogan on Quebec licence plates. It's a phrase to live by — a reminder of the differences that make the province special. And the phrase *Maitres chez nous*, used to propel Quebec into the modern era, was coined by a newspaper editor. Media play a big role in Quebec.

Maîtres chez nous (Masters of our own house)

- Do you believe that we live in a united Canada?
- Do you believe that our schools and our work, our economy and our politics have made us all pretty much the same?
- When you hear Québécois talk about their distinct society, do you roll your eyes and think that's an exaggeration?
- Then you probably haven't seen television or films from Quebec.

From its earliest days in North America, Quebec erected the "three pillars of survival," says Claude Bélanger, an historian at Marianopolis College in Montreal:

> In 1806, there started to appear, in Quebec City, a newspaper that was called *Le Canadien*. *Le Canadien* was of significance, at the time, because it was the first paper published in Canada entirely in French, and hence dedicated solely to the concerns of the francophone population, the cause of the reformers, and the survival of the Canadiens. Underneath the title, the newspaper outlined its motto or slogan: *Notre foi, notre langue, nos institutions* [our faith, our language, our institutions]. These three elements constituted essentially the three pillars of survival of French Canadians.[1]

With the Quiet Revolution, Quebec veered away from the Church and from many aspects of its social institutions, such as the deference to English business, the dominance of the family and its school system. What emerged was a cosmopolitan society with a powerful group of French capitalists and equally strong union and social justice movements. Most Québécois had gained a new confidence in themselves and the future. They were unique — and independence, or something like it, looked inevitable. Language remained the only one of the original three pillars left. That is why cultural productions based on language — the movies, TV and newspapers — became so important and why any discussion of Canadian media must recognize that fact.

But it would also be a mistake to think that all the old traditions have disappeared. Many of these have a way of living on, if only in memory or nostalgia, and thus they appear in Quebec's cultural artifacts. Sometimes the re-appearance gets enacted as a joke: in *C.R.A.Z.Y.*, for instance, when Zach, the young hero, imagines parishioners at his church singing Rolling Stones songs. Sometimes the institution of the close-knit family re-appears in the form of a hockey team, as in *Les Boys,* or in a remote mining community, as in *Mon oncle Antoine.*

Even in Quebec today there are social dynamics in play that differ from those in English Canada. For example, Quebec has gained control of its immigration system and gives preference to French speakers. This is particularly important because Quebec's birth-rate has fallen more than anywhere in Canada. Thus, new communities in Quebec include Haitians, other francophones from the Caribbean and Africans from several former French colonies. These groups usually feel comfortable settling in Quebec. Other immigrants, even when Catholic, have more difficulty if they prefer English schools for their children. Unfortunately, however, as in English Canada, Quebec's new demographic realities are not reflected in the Quebec media.

Quebec's union movement and groups working for social change remain among the strongest in North America. This undoubtedly reflects the traditions of community and social responsibility rather than the liberal individualism so prevalent in the U.S. and English Canada. In the dynamic years between 1960 and 1990, those who fought for independence believed that they were also creating a different, more socially democratic society. This no longer seems the case — Quebec nationalism and social democracy no longer walk hand-in-hand. But working-class organizations and many other political groups prevail. Even in the Canadian parliament, before the 2011 election, which decimated its numbers, the Bloc Québécois could be counted on as a social-democratic bulwark against the Conservative Party's agenda. Now, no doubt, that same concern is expected from the New Democratic Party.

The Two Founding Peoples

> Lord Durham wrote: "The English are superior to the French, not only by money but by intelligence. Ils devront toujours dominer le pays. [They will always rule the country.]"[2]

This reminder about the attitude of the governor general in 1838 was not written years ago in the heat of the independence movement but in 2010. The author, Lise Payette, is one of Quebec's leading journalists and a regular columnist for the prestigious newspaper *Le Devoir*. She continues,

> Le moins que l'on puisse dire, c'est que les Canadiens anglais ont de la suite dans les idées. [The least we can say is that English Canadians have the sequence of ideas.] La stratégie de Lord Durham est toujours à l'ordre du jour à Ottawa. [Lord Durham's strategy is still the agenda in Ottawa.] Si vous en doutiez, pensant qu'avec le temps le rapport de force avait évolué différemment, détrompez-vous: la volonté de Stephen Harper, énoncée il y a quelques jours et qui consiste à augmenter de 30 députés le nombre de représentants élus à la Chambre, est un autre pas vers la réalisation du rêve de Durham. [If you doubt it, thinking that over time the balance of power had evolved differently, think again: the will of Stephen Harper set out a few days ago consists of 30 members to increase the number of representatives elected to the House is another step towards realizing the dream of Durham.] L'objectif n'est pas seulement de rétablir l'équilibre entre les provinces, mais il s'agit encore

de soumettre le Bas-Canada et de diminuer le pouvoir du Québec, tout en restant dans les paramètres reconnus par l'Acte constitutionnel. [The goal is not only to restore the balance between provinces, but it remains… to diminish the power of Quebec….] Autrement dit, finir la job. [In other words, finish the job.]

Not everything in Quebec culture carries a political charge. As in English Canada, most people see their entertainment as a separate realm from politics. Even the day-to-day news remains either local or so momentous, like climate change or the Afghan war, as to be almost abstract. As in English Canada, Quebec's dominant media system mixes private corporations and federal or provincial media institutions. Support for so-called public broadcasting flows from Radio Canada and through the provincially funded Télé-Québec. Film and TV producers draw on Telefilm Canada ($25 million to sixteen projects in 2010) and other funding agencies.[3] In addition, Québécois have access to the private TV, radio and newspaper outlets of Quebecor, the radio and newspapers of Power Corporation and the independent commercial voice of *Le Devoir*. Like the rest of North America, TV is far and away the dominant source of news for most people, followed by newspapers and radio. Newspapers generate the most original news coverage and pull considerable weight with the business and government elites, so their influence far outweighs their readership.

Quebec has been changing along with the rest of Canada in two important ways. First its economy is connected more and more to global forces somewhat beyond its control. This means that international companies, including U.S. media giants, now increasing the flow through the internet, have more influence everywhere in Canada, but it also puts pressure on Quebec- and Canadian-based companies to expand outward. They become transnational and thus operate to some degree beyond the reach of any nation state.

Second, like much of the Western world, Quebec has become

Three Québécois Icons

In the Quebec mediascape, three icons hover above everything else: René Lévesque, Monique Leyrac and Celine Dion.

René Lévesque (1922–1987) first came to notice in the 1950s as a radio journalist with a wide following. As he moved into politics full-time he adopted Quebec independence as his life goal, and in the stunning election of 1976, became premier. Today, even beyond his death, Lévesque's name and example provide a measuring stick for all Quebec politics. Nothing on the national level escapes comparison with Lévesque.

Monique Leyrac is one of Quebec's greatest singers and actors. Her rendition of Gilles Vigneaults' "Mon Pays" in the 1960s linked her to the aspirations of Quebec sovereignty and made her world famous. "Monique Leyrac is unique. All subjects and all registers suit her. She makes transitions from French to English and from past to present with extraordinary ease.... Besides a voice and an intelligence she has at her command the skills of the actress" (*La Presse*, "Avec Monique Leyrac, une merveilleise soiree," March 26, 1966).

Celine Dion ranks as the biggest star that Quebec, or Canada, has ever produced. She was born poor, in the town of Charlemagne, the youngest of fourteen. But it is much more difficult to link her music with anything Québécois, politically or culturally. Her style is pure Las Vegas. To her fans, Celine's story exemplifies a local daughter with extraordinary talent who went out and conquered the world. To her detractors, Dion represents the globalization of music, a force that distorts local talent and traditions to create a homogenized, commercial sound and image. She has her babies in Florida and sings for the U.S. army in Iraq, but she maintains her home and roots in Quebec.

Cinema and TV

---

less insular and less ethnically defined by one or two groups. There is great and growing diversity within the province — through immigration and through the rising strength of First Nations, which draws it closer to Ontario and B.C. The political, social and cultural debates in Montreal, as in Toronto, no longer revolve around the same old problems. Progressive political and economic leaders, at least in the major cities, know that multiculturalism can be an incredible strength and resource. This puts them at odds with the reactionary agenda of the federal Conservative Party. Changing demographics also create ironic new realities. The largest religious group in Ontario is now Catholic, and many older immigrants wish to maintain their strong traditions of family values. In this sense Quebec no longer seems so unique in the Canadian sphere. In summary, Quebec culture, as reflected in and created in the media, shows marked differences from the rest of Canada. However, much is changing, so those differences maybe less clear-cut than thirty years ago.

The star system. That's one of the keys to Quebec's media success, said Guy Fournier in a report to Telefilm Canada in 2005. Film and TV actors in Quebec are not only talented and versatile, they are genuinely popular among all kinds of audiences. This, he says, is no accident: "To build up a star system, you need to believe in it and to have faith in your artists."[4]

Michel Côté, for example, has built a marvelous acting career in cinema, theatre and television playing serious as well as comic roles. "From affectionate rascal, to thoughtful and remorseful father and degenerate loner," writes Myriam Fontaine, "Michel Côté delivers a range of emotions that are regularly replenished in each film. Those that come to mind include *Cruising Bar* (1989), playing four different characters; *T'es belle Jeanne* (1989); *La vie après l'amour* (2000); *Sur le seuil* (2003); *Le dernier tunnel* (2004); the highly acclaimed *C.R.A.Z.Y.* (2005); and *Ma fille, mon ange* (2007).[5]

Roy Dupuis also exhibits great versatility. After becoming something of a national icon, the epitome of Quebec masculinity in earlier roles, his image later became more complicated. He played a gay prostitute in *Being at Home with Claude* (1991); the hockey legend, Maurice, Rocket, Richard in *The Rocket* (2006); and Romeo Dallaire, the Canadian general in Rwanda, in *Shake Hands with the Devil* (2008). The latter two films have become well-known to viewers of the English CBC.

Pascale Bussiers projects star power as well and is widely recognized for her continuing roles on TV in *Belle-Baie* (Radio-Canada, 2007–), a *téléroman* set in Acadian New Brunswick, and *Mirador* (2010), a drama about a public relations firm in Montreal. But it's her award-winning performance in *Alys Robi: My Life in Cinemascope* (Denise Filiatrault, 2004) that really shines. In it she plays the legendary Quebec singing star Alys Robi, who became a huge international star in the 1940s, then lost it all due to mental illness. The film shows the nearly forgotten tradition of Quebec's fabulously popular cabaret and vaudeville theatre in the 1930s and 1940s. And we also see how Alys Robi conquered the entertainment worlds of Toronto, Hollywood and England fifty years before Celine Dion.

Along with Quebec's star system, television drama continues its popularity because the series achieve long runs, many with hundreds of episodes. This obviously aids recognition of the actors but also allows production costs to be much lower than in English Canada and gives all involved a chance to really develop characters, storylines and marketing. At the box office, Quebec's films are much more successful than those of English Canada. For example, in 2005, Quebec films made up 12.4 percent of the box office in the province, whereas English Canadian films accounted for only 1.6 percent across the entire country. And in 2006, Quebec films made up 18 percent, that's one ticket in five, the best year ever. The average budget was $5 million.[6]

For many filmgoers around the world, the first films from Quebec in the 1970s stood out because they revealed the place to be very particular — set in North America but with an unusual culture. This in fact was the goal of many of the filmmakers, and they worked alongside others in different professions to create and build on the momentum of the Quiet Revolution. *Mon oncle Antoine,* produced by Claude Jutra and Michel Brault in 1971, tells the story of several characters in a small mining town during the 1940s. It combines realist period detail with the fantastic and walks the fine line between fond remembrance and a not-so-pleasant milieu of the old Quebec. For many viewers, the film carries great poignancy because it depicts the years just before Quebec's mine workers had gathered the strength to take on the big Canadian and U.S. mining companies. *Kamouraska* and *J.A. Martin, Photographie* (Beaudin, 1976) looked much further back to the nineteenth century. These were costume pictures that staked a claim to a Quebec history that was both complex and sophisticated. They stood out as well by placing the concerns of its women characters in the foreground, which also made them modern in their sensibilities. Although these films, and others like them, were set in a pre-industrial society, they made the point that Quebec was much more than Catholic peasant farmers.

But Quebec also developed its own genres and forms of TV. The two most successful series, apart from its children's shows, have been *Les Plouffe* (1953–1959) and *Les Boys* (2007), both produced by Radio Canada. *La famille Plouffe* (*The Plouffe Family*) was based on a 1948 novel by Roger Lemelin. It immediately became the hit of the 1950s in the new genre of *téléroman* (similar but somewhat different from U.S. soap operas or Spanish *telenovelas*). It was live TV and ran for 194 episodes. The series was revived again with films and another *téléroman* in the 1980s. Unlike the glamourous and wealthy U.S. soap characters, the Plouffes are a working-class extended family from a poor district of Quebec City. Although the series often deals with hardships and tragic moments in the years following the Second World War, the general tone is light, often comic. Many of the actors became stars in Quebec, well-known to millions. The series also played in English CBC but "modifications were made in the script to remove profane and vulgar language and any references to sex."[7]

Les Boys (Louis Saia) began in 1997 as a wildly successful film and then spun-off in 2007 as a *téléroman*. Upon its release in Quebec, *Les Boys* was met with an overwhelmingly negative response from critics, but the film was embraced by the public. The series features an amateur hockey team, with middle-aged players from many professions — a doctor, a mechanic, a gay lawyer, etc. Everyone is stereotyped, the plots are obvious formulas and the tone is farce, somewhat in the tradition of French theatre. There's plenty of slapstick, sports comedy and sexual innuendo. The same applies to *Cruising Bar* (Ménard, 1989) and *Cruising Bar 2* (2009), where popular actor Michel Côté plays four different Montreal male types taken to outrageous exaggeration — the boring playboy, the pimply nerd, the horny auto dealer and the wigged-out rocker. It's a cross between classical French farce and "stupid" comedy in the vein of Adam Sandler.

Although the TV version of *Les Boys* was made for Radio-Canada, the place for such low-brow fare is usually TVA, Quebec's most popular network. TVA draws the largest audiences for its homegrown reality/talent shows, such as *Star Académie* (2003–), and for a host of cruder, commercial rations of talk-shows and reality TV. This success should remind us that much of Quebec popular culture remains totally conventional, trading in stereotypes and traditional prejudices against outsiders. However, the producer of *Star Académie*, Julie Snyder, perhaps the most powerful TV producer in Canada, argues that her shows are different than elsewhere. "In Quebec, the people who are on TV are like part of the family. *American Idol* couldn't exist here because it humiliates people. *Star Académie* wasn't like that. It was there to help family life, to get people around their televisions rooting for contestants from all over Quebec. It was like Sunday mass."[8] Nevertheless, it is TVA's parent owner, Quebecor, that has created the country's most right-wing TV network, Sun TV. And Snyder's common-law partner is Pierre Karl Peladeau, the president of Quebecor.

A much more sophisticated work that also plays with social types is the film *C.R.A.Z.Y.* (2005), directed by Jean-Marc Vallée. It tells the story of a working-class family in Montreal during the 1960s and 1970s. The parents have five sons ("A surplus of male hormones," says the father, played with great subtlety by Michel Côté), all different and all clear types — the egghead, the jock, the criminal, the baby and the anguished Zach, who is struggling with his sexual identity. To come out as a gay teenager in such a family at such a time definitely takes courage. The conventional world of factory work, hockey, summer camp, high-school brawling just doesn't work for Zach. As is common in many contemporary films, the director provides a lightly mixed genre salad, combining drama, fantasy and several layers of comedy. We laugh at Zach's conflicts with his brothers and little misunderstandings with his father. The father is not a brute and he has his doubts about the value of the Catholic Church, but he loves his sons. The problem is his rigid idea of manhood based in a working-class version of the culture-at-large and the Church. Ironically, but perhaps typically for film, Zach's mother is much more devout than her husband but also much more understanding of boys. She does not have to uphold her identity to be sympathetic to Zach's sensitive side. In fact she thinks he has a gift of being able to affect events for the good. The story unfolds through flashback from Zach's point-of-view.

The setting for *C.R.A.Z.Y.* is unmistakable. A viewer knowing nothing going into the film would have no difficulty recognizing Quebec's particular mix of cultural elements. Big American cars washed in the driveway every Saturday, mass on Sunday, summer camp in the woods, René Lévesque on TV, and hockey, hockey, hockey. A Catholic Tupperware woman can see into the future. The soundtrack combines Patsy Cline, David Bowie, Charles Aznavour and Quebec disco. Both father and son rely heavily on music as a place of refuge and as an avenue to a larger world of much broader horizons. The father has his Patsy Cline and Charles Aznavour, which provide both nostalgia and the glimpse of a more romantic life. Zach has Pink Floyd and Bowie to himself, where the family will not follow him; but the music also represents a larger world beyond confined, working-class Quebec.

C.R.A.Z.Y. works with the forms of contemporary world cinema, edited for speed and with leaps and bounds from one year to the next. Single sequences take us from one era to the next as a matter of course. And by using the flashback device, Vallée is able to mix realism and the fantastic of memories. Zach's voice-over also provides plenty of opportunity for ironic comedy and sarcastic statements that contradict the images onscreen. At one point Zach recalls that his family "always ate gourmet meals" as we see heaping plates of deviled eggs and celery filled with Cheez Whiz.

Raymond, the bad brother, carries the hate for Zach the furthest — he lives in the basement recreation room where he smokes dope and maintains a non-stop sex-life. His hatred, violence and criminal record remind us that 1970s Quebec had its nasty undercurrent. This keeps the film from becoming overly romantic about the cultural changes then taking place. It's noteworthy that Raymond displays a Parti Québécois flag in his basement room, a sign of a movement that was still on the outside of power looking in. There are no other signs of Quebec politics in the film.

C.R.A.Z.Y. is also a somewhat typical coming-of-age / coming-out story, addressed to twenty-something viewers. Perhaps for that reason, despite its Quebec-ness, the film has travelled well internationally and maintains a steady life via DVD rentals. It walks the fine line between mainstream entertainment and the art house. The particular aspects of Quebec life, the matter-of-fact gay-positive approach and the way in which Vallée pushes the boundaries of scene and narrative construction take it out of the mainstream. It is the quirky specificity however — the little details of working-class Montreal — that art house audiences crave. For these viewers the more specific and detailed the local content, the more universal its appeal. This is the polar opposite of the uniformity of dominant cinema. *C.R.A.Z.Y.* exhibits high quality work all around, with skilled acting, especially from Michel Côté, Zach's father. It took Vallée ten years to raise the $7 million budget. It proved very popular in Quebec, was a critical hit world-wide and made decent profits.

Box-office success is important for the funders of feature fiction in Canada, but so is international prestige and popular entertainment in a Canadian vein. For this reason viewers will continue to be presented with *Les Boys* on one screen and the latest art film on another. If neither makes boffo box-office, their federal funders will have covered their backsides. Films that are genuinely popular, critically acclaimed and make a small profit, such as *C.R.A.Z.Y.*, represent the golden egg — tantalizing but seldom seen.

A newer trend of art films have been labelled the Quebec New

Wave. These are directed by young Québécois who seem to have lost interest in the questions of independence. The film critic Patricia Bailey describes their new orientation: "While the characters speak French, their experience as members of North America's largest francophone minority barely registers. Their cultural reference points are universally North American, not specific to Quebec. Questions of language and nation are conspicuously absent."[9] Films such as Stéphane Lafleur's Continental, un film sans fusil (*Continental, a Film without Guns*, 2008) depicts suburban singles who have taken up the very American phenomenon of line dancing. *Tout est parfait* by Yves-Christian Fournier (2008) tells the story of five young people who make a collective suicide pact. *Derriere moi* by Rafaël Ouellet (2008) portrays adolescent prostitution in a small town.

Bailey observes that in these somber and dark films there is little of the stereotypical good humour and family warmth that many viewers associate with Quebec film. But these are films with small audiences — it would be a mistake to see their approach as a popular trend. They do however reflect some of the feelings of young Quebec intellectuals who in earlier generations saw more potential in political movements of social change.

Quebec's Radical Film Tradition

Throughout the years 1960 to 1995, Quebec's artists and filmmakers combined their desire for sovereignty (or independence) with radical social and economic change. A free Quebec should also be a different Quebec, they believed.[10] Thus, a long tradition of working-class subjects, feminism, Aboriginal issues and many other pressing concerns of society has shaped modern Quebec cinema. These films serve to complicate any easy notions of Quebec nationalism. First off they raise issues of class and the status of women. They also raise issues such as place — what are the boundaries of Quebec and how were they established; history — when did Quebec and the Québécois come into existence, replacing New France and French Canada; and identity — who is us — what about First Nations and allophones and new immigrants, and those of mixed parents?[11]

In 1956, the NFB moved its offices from Ottawa to Montreal, partly to gain more independence from the government, and by 1959, a new "French Unit" was making ground-breaking work, some of it closely aligned with the new political movements in Quebec. For example, Arthur Lamothe's *Bucherons de la Monouane* (1962) employed many elements of political documentary, including "research, analysis of a particular situation (working conditions and life in lumber camps in Northern Quebec), and information… given in an 'off-screen' commentary, which had a didactic and a political function."[12]

Some filmmakers looked at the rural traditions and experiences of working people — *Les Raquetteurs* (Gilles Groulx, Michel Brault, Marcel Carriere, 1959), the world-famous documentary on a winter carnival in Sherbrooke, *Pour la suite du monde* (Pierre Perrault and Michel Brault, 1963),[13] on beluga fishing communities on the Saint Lawrence, *Jean Carignan: violoneux* (Bernard Gosselin, 1975) and many others. Most of these films were well-received for their warmth and quality, but some critics hated what they saw as a romantic look backward. They called them folkloric and reactionary. Michel Euvard and Pierre Véronneau wrote: "This desire to return to one's roots in order to take stock of them is not limited to Quebec; it is characteristic of all nations which have been repressed." A brilliant, later film called *La Turlutte* [*The Ballad of Hard Times*] (Pascal Gélinas and Richard Boutet, 1983) looks back at the depression years of the 1930s in rural Quebec. It is neither folkloric in the usual sense nor reactionary. With great verve and energy, it manages to analyze the economic situation and reveal how events affected people directly. There is little narration; instead most of the people interviewed sing songs that tell their stories.

Others working at the NFB/ONF in the 1960s and 1970s took up the cause of the industrial and service workers. The result was clearly radical and caused uneasiness among business and government elites. In addition to Denys Arcand's controversial *On es ou cotton*

(1970), about the textile industry, Arthur Lamothe's *Le mepris n'aura qu'un temps* (1973) is a powerful and angry film about accidents in the booming construction industry and Maurice Bulbulian's *Richesse des autres* (1973), on the mining industry, compares the local situation to that of Chile. These films were informed as much by Marxism and anti-colonialism as by any fascination with Quebec culture. This focus on the province's staple industries — textiles, lumber, fishing, and mining — has continued by producers working with the ONF or independently. For example, Sohpie Bissonnette's (b. 1956) film *Lea Roback: A Vision in the Darkness* (1992) portrays the labour leader, anti-fascist and feminist. Roback was famous for her organizing work among textile workers. She also led a major strike at the Montreal factories of RCA Victor, the giant U.S. company that dominated the radio and recording industry.

Tahani Rached, originally from Egypt, has produced an impressive body of work known partly for its depiction of immigrant communities in Quebec, such as *Les voleurs de jobs* (1979). Her more recent films take us into the lives of women and girls in Egypt, Lebanon, Haiti and Palestine. These not only help to explain the dreadful conflicts in those countries but provide insight into the roots of many of Quebec's newest immigrants.

Quebec's filmmakers have also produced some of the most radical political fiction in North America. These have tackled not only local or passing problems but the basic foundations of Quebec society. Denys Arcand's *Rejeanne Padovani* (1973) weaves a suspenseful tale, certainly based on reality, of corruption involving provincial politicians, the construction industry, organized crime and unions. It reflects Arcand's bitter outlook, but it was a story that needed to be told. Michel Brault's *Les Ordes* (1974) takes its cue from the events of the October Crisis of 1970. The film mixes the conventions of documentary and narrative fiction and shows the trauma inflicted on people arrested without reason or charges, as happened in Montreal after the Trudeau government declared martial law. It reveals just how thin is the veneer of human rights in modern Canada.[14]

Pierre Falardeau (1946–2009) was a much more polemical, at times crude, political filmmaker. In his *Speak White* (1980) he created a rapid, in-your-face collage which linked anti-Black racism with the common English insult that Québécois speak English. In *Octobre* (1994) he told the story of the FLQ crisis from the point-of-view of an FLQ cell. And in his most famous work, *Elvis Gratton* (1981), he satirized those Quebec federalists whose life goal is to win fame as an Elvis impersonator. *Polytechnique* (2009) by Denis Villeneuve, is a dramatization of the 1989 "Montreal Massacre," in which fourteen women students were killed by a lone gunman. While the film has been criticized for its narrow focus, showing only the immediate events, thus refraining from drawing any conclusions or pointing to larger issues, it remains important for keeping the event in the public eye. This is especially needed in this age when feminism and gun control are so often characterized as passé or unnecessary.

Some producers combined their portraits of Quebec with films of international solidarity. Foremost was Yvan Patry (1948–1999), who with his partner Daniele Lacourse struggled for thirty years often in very dangerous situations — Eritrea, Nicaragua, Mexico and above all Rwanda. They were the only Western filmmakers in Rwanda in the days immediately following the genocide of 1994. Their three-part masterpiece, *Chronicle of a Genocide Foretold*, documented for the first time those atrocities, but also Canadian involvement, the failure of the superpowers and the role of General Romeo Dallaire. This work was so intense that it undoubtedly led to Patry's early death. The foundation AlterCiné was set up in his honour to support filmmakers who continue this work. Producers from Peru, Cameroon, Lebanon, India and many other countries have benefited. [15]

Others, such as Helene Klodawsky, of Montreal, have made extraordinary works, such as *No More Tears Sister: Anatomy of Hope and Betrayal* (2004), about a Sri Lankan feminist and civil rights activist assassinated in 1989, and *Family Motel* (2007), about the struggles of Somali refugees in Ottawa. The film reviewer Matthew Hays reminds us that political filmmakers keep challenging their audiences through new forms of storytelling: "Klodawsky straddles one heckuva high-wire act with *Family Motel*; she's managed to look back at some of the very best documentary-drama hybrids from the NFB's storied past, while looking forward, incorporating our culture's newer baggage involving reality TV and the new face of poverty."[16]

Newspapers
Le Devoir, La Presse, The Gazette

A comparison of the Montreal papers *Le Devoir* and *La Presse* demonstrates how their news coverage differs from that in the rest of Canada, showing that the days of partisan editorializing never really

---

Quebec Newspapers (in order of circulation)

Le Journal de Montreal 1964. Largest tabloid in Canada; largest French-language paper in North America (Wikipedia). Owned by Sun Media (Quebecor). Circulation 214,000 daily.

La Presse. 1884. Broadsheet. Generally federalist. Owned by Groupe Gesca, a subsidiary of Power Corporation of Canada. Circulation 212,000 daily.

Gazette. 1778. Broadsheet. Only English-language daily. Owned by Postmedia Network Inc.
Circulation 163,000 daily

Le Devoir (duty) Founded by Henri Bourassa in 1910. Nationalist orientation. Independent.
Circulation: weekdays 35,000; Saturday 58,000

"To ensure the triumph of ideas over appetites, of the public good over partisan interests, there is but one means: awake in the people, and above all in the ruling classes, a sense of public duty in all its forms: religious duty, national duty, civic duty."
— Henri Bourassa.

The Quebec Liberal Party campaigned successfully in the significant 1960 election under the slogans *Maîtres chez nous* [Masters of our own house] and *Il faut que ça change* [Things have to change], phrases coined by *Le Devoir* editor Andre Laurendeau.

The Society for News Design has called *Le Devoir* the world's most beautiful newspaper.

ended, as the official newspaper histories claim. *Le Devoir* supports Quebec sovereignty, while *La Presse* supports Canadian federalism. *Le Devoir* is owned by its employees; *La Presse* by the Power Corporation, a large transnational group with strong ties to the Liberal Part of Canada.

The *Le Devoir* front page for October 2, 2010, featured a large colour reproduction of *Le vieux patriote*, the iconic painting of a nineteenth-century rebel habitant carrying a rifle. This image inspired the FLQ in 1970. The *La Presse* front page for the same day showed a large colour collage featuring a Canadian soldier patrolling the streets of Montreal during the imposition of the War Measures Act in October 1970. The Headline is "Octobre Noir."

As for the federalist *Gazette*, an issue from that week included a lengthy review of new book on Pierre Trudeau, a photo of Opposition Leader Michael Ignatieff, with the caption "Ignatieff tears into sovereignists," and a strong rebuttal of a *Macleans* article claiming that the number one province for corruption is Quebec. An editorial from the same period had this to say: "It's time for Quebec to rethink its relationship with its English-speaking minority. English-speaking Quebecers are not a threat to the majority. Au contraire, English-speaking Quebecers have made — and continue to make — enormous contributions to Quebec society in every walk of life, from education and business to health and agriculture, not to mention science, technology and the arts."[17]

Quebec newspapers often seem to operate in a hothouse of concentrated debate. We might look, for example, at the media frenzy over "reasonable accommodation" toward immigrants, especially whether Muslim women should be allowed to wear veils or burqas in public. The prominent journalist Chantal Hébert argues: "By the sheer nature of its size and its relative homogeneity, francophone Quebec is home to a journalism of proximity that translates into a capacity to mobilize public opinion in ways unparalleled anywhere else in Canada."[18]

Special Debates

When citizens of Quebec turn to serious newspapers, radio and TV they find debates about issues not seen in English Canada. Some of the stories and editorials that regularly appear deal with the following concerns.

Quebec's relationship to Canada in general and the federal government particularly occupy centre stage in the press. These controversies range far beyond the kinds of discussions held between other provinces and Ottawa. The stakes are high. For example: Does Quebec have the right leave Canada, according to international law? Does Quebec give more than it gets from Canada? What's the goal for those who want to change the status quo — complete independence, a new deal in Canada or some type of sovereignty-association? Does an independent Quebec mean a different Quebec, in terms of social relations, class relations and economics? Will an independent Quebec make its citizens more vulnerable to the U.S., for example, more reliant on water and energy exports?

The place of First Nations takes on added urgency in Quebec. What if, for example, Aboriginal peoples living in Quebec do not want to leave Canada? Most Canadians can ignore Aboriginal people, but those pushing for Quebec independence must work out a specific relationship immediately. What are the boundaries of Quebec: those which were defined during the French Regime, those defined at Confederation or those vast areas that have since been added, such as the far North? The answer to this directly affects any negotiations between the First Nations and Quebec.

A third set of high-stakes debates centres on Quebec's traditional culture versus the various manifestations of modern culture. Should we celebrate the old traditions, which show us to be obviously different, or do those folkloric images hold us back? Does independence mean a more global, cosmopolitan culture, which could overwhelm the French language and specific Quebec traditions? In recent years these questions have centred on the specific ideology of "reasonable accommodation." In other words, how should Québécois culture deal with the cultural norms of its immigrant communities.

To sum up, Quebec's media share many characteristics with the rest of Canada, fundamentally in its mix of capitalist and state institutions. In addition, its managers and creative people occupy the same social and demographic features — well educated, middle-class, predominantly male and white. At the same time Quebec has carved out a very different media world, which has enjoyed both massive popularity and financial stability. Both the entertainment and the news media in Quebec play an ever larger role in the development of the present society. For Guy Fournier, "Television has done nothing less than enable the emergence of an 'instant' culture in Quebec.... Before television there was no culture in Quebec, there was only folklore."[19]

5. THE NEW MEDIA

While the new right soaks in the opiate of religion,
The new liberals inhale deeply from the opiate of technology.

New media usually refers to all those creative forms that use digital technology embedded in a wide range of computer and communication devices.[1] These include the internet and all forms of social media, such as Facebook, YouTube, messaging, etc. Because digital processes allow information to be broken down into tiny bits, new media excel in the creation of multi-media forms, using text, images, video and sound. New media encourage the transfer of one media form into another. They are interactive, permitting two-way or multiple communication. They allow everyone to be a creator, not simply a passive spectator. They can be delivered to a mass audience around the world or to very specific groups. To their proponents, they will overthrow or radically change all of the old media. Most of this, of course, is nonsense. The only thing certain is that new media are digitally based and encourage multi-media forms. Everything else remains potential or utopian wishful thinking.

Like television and radio before then, these technologies have arrived with enormous expectations. For nationalists, they provide a chance for many more Canadian voices to be heard in the global village and for Canadians in all sorts of communities to know each other. For business, these technologies have great potential for both marketing and sales, also a chance to break beyond borders and join the race to globalization. For governments and economists, they promise thousands of jobs. For educators, new media make distance learning and flexible, online learning a reality. For believers in traditional, high culture, they provide another chance to bring the world's great culture to the masses, an opportunity that failed in the wasteland of television. For political activists, they hold great possibilities for out-flanking the dominant media, in order to reach Canadians directly, or to form coalitions with new ideas for social change.

One Toronto business consultant who believes in the world of new media is Don Tapscott. In his book *Growing Up Digital*, he claims to make "a compelling distinction between the passive medium of television and explosion of interactive digital media, sparked by the computer and the Internet." Children, he says, "empowered by new technology, are taking the reins from their boomer parents and making inroads into all areas of society, including our education system, the government, and economy."[2]

Unfortunately, the experience of teachers and other new media analysts runs counter to Tapscott's claims. A large number of young people may be growing up surrounded by new media and proficient in some of its forms, but most of their skills remain narrow and shallow — confined to chatting, texting, shopping and YouTube surfing.[3] A significant number will go on to be skilled, creative and powerful but this will be the result of hard work, family and class advantage, and a good education.

Unlike the older arts, the modern media cannot exist without elaborate electronic machinery at all phases of production and exhibition. These technologies exist almost solely as industrial products based on advanced science, engineering and precision, large-scale manufacturing. Each stage in the media flow — production and recording, distribution and reception — requires a different set of technologies. In these ways technology shapes the art and shapes the audience, for example, its size and its experience. But how do these technologies come into being?

The past ten years have seen many new technologies, which in turn have partly spawned new types of communication. The mobile phone in particular, following a new round of miniaturization, has allowed millions in the world's poorest countries to communicate. And in the rich world, handheld devices could very well push the personal computer itself to the margins. Miniaturization and increased capacity in computer, telephone and satellite systems has also brought us Facebook, Twitter, the iPhone, and the latest tablet devices.

New technologies tend to be both welcomed and feared. Some make communication easier or enrich our experience; others just complicate our lives or throw us out of work. But, whether positive or negative, they are never made in the laboratory one day and the next let loose upon the world. Media historian Brian Winston studied the sequence whereby technologies come into our lives, and he shows that, in every case, the new device has unfolded over a period of years, even decades. This calls into question the modern idea of a sudden technological revolution.[4] Machines or devices only become diffused once a strong social, economic or political need for them exists. In addition, citizens and workers can occasionally apply the brakes, especially when new technology means job losses, speed-up at the workplace and surveillance.

Technology promises us revolutions. On the contrary, however, most of the new media and communication forms have clearly not transformed the key social and economic relations firmly entrenched since the nineteenth century. We may have entered the shiny new world of digital capitalism, but it's still capitalism. "Digital capitalism has strengthened, rather than banished, the age-old scourges of the market system: inequality and domination."[5]

When we consider the complex and usually drawn-out introduction of new media forms it becomes harder to think of technology as the only factor for change. Modern technology can certainly prove either disruptive or liberating, but it does not unfold in a vacuum and it seldom functions as the lone motor driving the media forward. A better way to understand the effects of media technology is through its various relationships, for example, with the economics of the media industries — their use of technology, costs, efficiency and labour.

New Technology

From the 1990s on, people started to distinguish new media from old media. New media comprised all those forms based on computers. For those of us on the receiving end, the CD-ROM provided a first taste, followed in rapid succession by the networking of computers, web pages, online magazines, radio and films and the ubiquitous mobile phones and Blackberrys. But this active, interactive, open source world of new possibilities, which encourages us to see ourselves as producers of art or communicators of useful information, now coexists, especially on the internet, with more passive activities of listening to, reading and watching what others have produced. Many of those others include the largest commercially driven media firms, such as Bell, Rogers and the like. New media often seem to come to us primarily as user-friendly consumer appliances — smaller, cheaper and smarter at every turn. Standing just behind them, however, is the rather daunting science of broadband communication, data compression, hi-speed relays and switching, transponders and the wireless universe of satellites (propelled into space, lest we forget, by billion-dollar rockets).

Many people believe that the new media technologies have led us to a new economy, a new politics and new social relations. If the old economy was dominated by the ghost of Henry Ford and his assembly line for mass production of industrial goods, many observers believe that a new post-Fordist economy is upon us. In this new era, workers need not congregate in large factories, and production tends toward flexible specialization. Because the old mass markets are fragmenting, media companies must restructure to produce specialized or customized products for particular markets. This accurately captures the world of the largest multi-media conglomerates in the West. It is less accurate if we look at the rest of the world. India, the Philippines and Korea have encouraged the creation of large media factories for animation and software production, assembly-lines for the TV and computer giants. For these countries, and the managers and workers of the operations, flexibility seems a distant goal.

Diverse, Better Societies

If the old Canadian politics relied on masses and classes linked in cities and regions, new media, it is said, pushes us toward more diversity, the development of communities of interest beyond the old borders and a concern over the effects of globalization. But it is just as true that new media may have widened the existing class divide, even in Canada, where the costs of cable, satellite receiving and the internet are well out of reach for many.

Proponents of new media come in all political stripes. In addition to the elites, led by Google's Sergey Brin and News Corp's Rupert Murdoch and egged on by business writers like Don Tapscott, who tout technology as a way forward for Canadian capitalism, many people working for democracy and social change profess high hopes as well. Take the bloggers. To blog is to create and maintain a regular, online diary or weblog, comprised of ideas, stories, manifestos and above all, links to other peoples' weblogs.

"Journalism," says one blogger, "is being revolutionized by the latest technology. We have gone from Old Media, through New Media, to We Media: the idea of using the power and the knowledge and the energy of people at the edges." As British journalist Ben Hammersley reports: "Because bloggers on similar subjects link to each other, the reader finds it easier to understand opposing points of view. On the internet, everyone is the same size — and by allowing experts in their field to correct others and be corrected themselves, almost in real time, blogs release the voice of the readership."[6]

So, let's leave aside the self-promotion and utopian dreams and focus on the realities. Online news sources have multiplied substantially since 2000, and the internet buzzes with predictions about the death of old news media. As computer use accelerates and fast broadband connections become widely available, media companies are changing the way the news is delivered. Not only that: citizens of all kinds have begun to write, report and distribute news of their own.

The special features of the internet have the potential to change many characteristics of news itself, opening up fresh possibilities and creating broader expectations about journalism. In fact, the newest online forms, especially the social networking media such as Facebook, YouTube and Twitter, now work as important news conduits, especially for young people. And because these sites connect like-minded people, it seems to many of their users that the social media operate separately from the dominant news media. Users can simply move on when authorities or blatantly commercial operators move in.

All this poses an enormous challenge to the dominant news business. Some editors and journalists in TV, print and radio react with fear or scorn. They contend that these new "amateur" forms of news, where anyone can voice an opinion and no one steps forward to edit, will discredit all journalism. Others claim that great amounts of online material, written and posted exclusively by one person, can't be trusted. Only the well-established institutions, they say — such as the CBC, with its internal checks and balances — can be relied on to report serious and complex issues and be held accountable for what they produce.

But not everyone in the dominant media views online news as a threat. Many in the business see the potential of extending the reach of the old companies. Esther Enkin, acting editor in chief of the CBC *News Editors' Blog* believes this to be so: "We hope the *Editors' Blog* will be yours as much as ours. This is a place for us to have a conversation with you about what we do, how we do it and why we do it. We hope to explain, and explore, the editorial dilemmas that face us as a public broadcaster in this exciting, ever changing modern media environment…. This is a logical extension of our role as public broadcasters…. It is our job to foster an ongoing dialogue about what matters to Canadians. The world of the web has only made that discussion more immediate, challenging and thorough."[7] Yet this is surely an overstatement about democratic trends in media. Clearly, a reporter for a major news outfit, such as the *Vancouver Sun* or *La Presse*, carries the enormous power and clout of a dominant institution. And company connections provide a guest pass to places of power that would be closed to the average do-it-yourself online journalist.

Defenders of the dominant media argue that the internet provides space for everyone to express their views, communicate their cultural values and create their own stories. At the same time many strong critics of the dominant media argue that the internet allows us to receive and transmit information and ideas without all the gatekeepers who populate the mainstream media. For many of its promoters, this online media world is a positive symbol of globalization and the competitive capitalist system, demonstrating that almost anyone can jump into the media game. These defenders of the dominant media believe that Marshall McLuhan's 1960s prediction of a global village has finally come to pass. Not only can we receive information from far away, but we can speak and work with others directly, no matter how distant their homes.

The Demise of Old Media?

Those who concoct the arguments about the death of old media make for some strange bedfellows. Many believe simply that newspapers are the bastion of democracy in the West, without them the government and unruly citizens would run amok. These folks don't seem to understand that the news media play an absolutely crucial role in the running of the modern state. The Canadian government and ruling elites need the *Globe and Mail* and CTV news as sources of information for themselves and to communicate to the public. The state will never allow these organs to disappear — just as the U.S. banks were described in the crisis of 2009 as "too big to fail." The media business works like no other. Profits are essential but so too are the political relationships and connections that accompany an organization that provides an essential service.

Another group that exaggerates the fall of old media is comprised of the internet utopians, who wish and assume that new media will soon take over. These are the people who announce that "everyone's online now," "nobody reads such an old-fashioned (dead-tree) medium as newspapers anymore" — as if social class has simply dissolved. The 2010 U.K. general election showed clearly that TV debates count far more than anything new media can generate. Unfortunately, many young, well-educated urban leftists fall under this utopian category. Many have come to believe that they are a "net generation," very different from those who came before.[8] Because their experience centres on the internet's alternative information sites they assume that the rest of the country will soon follow suit and that old media, like a tired geranium, will die from lack of attention. But, if they're looking for the imminent fall of the dominant media, they'll have a long wait.

Perhaps the most powerful of the exaggerators are the computer industry giants with big systems and small gizmos to sell — their players and pods, e-readers and pads, created they say to sweep us into an egalitarian future. Many colleges and universities eagerly promote this "everyone is wired" ideology, as do Canada's federal government and its allies in the telecommunications business, such as BCE, Rogers, Alliant and the like. As we'll see later, however, the facts speak otherwise.

News Sources

Despite what we may think of the promises made by the advocates of online news and entertainment, this newly emerging digital world does contain exciting characteristics that set it apart from older forms. Online media have the potential to combine different forms of communication — text, sounds and images. In addition, although still rare, some online news sites allow users to speak and listen to others in real time, to carry on real conversations. Although the term "interactive" has been shamelessly hyped, especially by those who sell computers and software, the world of online communication does provide opportunities for two-way conversations. No longer need we be passive consumers of what the experts deem newsworthy or entertaining. We can talk back. We can also modify the forms by which we receive these media, for example, through customized news feeds and alerts. Finally, we have the ability to create and distribute our own stories that might reach many, many people.

Simply by clicking on a standard source such as Google News, anyone has access to hundreds of articles from newspapers all over the world, many we've never heard of, let alone read. A slightly more knowledgeable web surfer can draw on archives, blogs, podcasts, wikis, maps and image banks from photojournalists to gather information and opinions far beyond the dominant sources. For example, English Canadians interested in the culture and news of Quebec can read the *Montreal Mirror* or *Le Devoir* online, with instant, albeit crude, translation, and then link to hundreds of other articles.

Online news has been developed by two types of organizations: the *new groups*, which have created stand-alone websites and the *established media* companies, which have developed specialized news sites or online versions of their existing newspapers, television stations and radio networks. Websites created by new organizations on the left include the outstanding rabble.ca and RealNews, in Toronto, Tyee, in Vancouver, and the Centre for Media Alternatives, in Montreal. Others, such as the *Dominion*, based in Ottawa, and *Redwire Media* in

Two Alternative Magazines

The *Dominion*

The consolidation of corporate control and ownership in Canada has resulted in a decrease in investigative journalism, an increase in the number of stories journalists are expected to produce and a narrowing in the range of debate on key issues of importance. The *Dominion* aims to widen the range of debate by covering stories marginalized, spun, or simply ignored by the mainstream press. As an independent publication relying primarily on *reader support* rather than advertisers, the *Dominion* represents a new model of newspaper in Canada, created unambiguously for the public good, rather than for maximizing profit.

The *Dominion*'s aim is not just to report that something is the case, but to examine *why* it is the case. By providing context to stories, and giving voice to perspectives that are marginalized and those most affected by events or decisions, the *Dominion* hopes to promote understanding through accurate, in-depth reporting.

Redwire Media

We are a collective of Native youth creating uncensored spaces for youth to find their own voice. All of our media projects are initiated and led by youth, inspiring creativity, confidence, motivation and action. Our goals are to:

- offer opportunities for youth to learn practical skills in media
- facilitate community access to film, print, radio, podcasting, websites and performance
- create space for Native youth to educate each other on the issues facing their communities
- support and promote Native youth artists, writers, activists, performers and musicians
- encourage creativity and critical perspectives.

Sources: <www.dominionpaper.ca>, <redwiremag.com>.

Vancouver, published small magazines first but have been able to expand considerably by moving online.

Extending the Old Media

Existing media organizations with websites include the CBC, all the commercial broadcasters and most of the major newspapers. In the case of Postmedia, the site canoe.ca hosts all the newspapers and other media outlets connected to their corporate chain. These new sources of news range from sites with very large readerships to organizations with tiny audiences. The biggest operate around the clock while the smallest publish on a magazine schedule, with new content usually added weekly. Some sites created by old-media owners, such as the *Globe and Mail*, provide a new type of service and include original content. But many others simply dump their regular stories into the site. This goes by the derogatory name of "shovel-ware" in the business. Many small radio, newspaper and television outlets operate this way.

The aggregator sites — Google, in particular — are truly innovative. Although none of them have their own journalists, they bring together and juxtapose news from a range of sources, then rank and display it, often creating startling forms of fresh knowledge. When you have the *Globe and Mail* and the *Daily Champion* of Lagos, Nigeria, both reporting on the same story, you can get a wider and deeper perspective on things. The presence of Google in Canada helps citizens link to dozens of new Canadian sources, but in general, and in keeping with the other commercial media, Google acts as a funnel for even more U.S. content.

The old groups still dominate: the CBC, the *Globe and Mail*, the *Vancouver Sun*, *Macleans*, etc. And, as we have seen, the new kid online, Sun TV, flows from the second largest media group in the country, Quebecor. Elsewhere on the right, a growing number of sites, with growing audiences, include the *Western Standard*, which began life as a newspaper but has since morphed into a website.

Blogs

A growing number of online news sources stretch the boundaries of news and push the differences from traditional media much further.

In particular, the blog, a type of journal combined with links and comments, has gained so much attention that the word itself has spawned offspring, such as blogger and blogosphere, the "place" where blogging takes place.

The concept of a journal or diary, actually an old form, implies something casual, often conversational in tone. It allows a personal voice and often features impressions rather than verifiable facts or a tightly argued essay. Many blogs function as simple diaries, with short blasts of opinion, neither of which qualify as news. The best provide a running commentary on current events and function as a remarkable resource, like a helpful librarian or hip sister — making links and connections or pointing out untapped sources of information. There are three main types of blog, each delivering what I'd define as news: pundit blogs, participant blogs and citizen journalists online.

Pundits

Well-known old-media pundits and journalists, such as Mark Steyn, of *Macleans* magazine and Andrew Coyne, of the *National Post*, use blogs to extend their substantial reach. *Macleans*, the country's only national newsmagazine, which is owned by the giant Rogers, actively promotes its six bloggers — all white men.

Prominent right-wing blogging includes both old and new pundits. Paul Wells, of *Macleans*, often ranks as the country's number one blogger. Catherine McMillan's *The Roadkill Diaries*, from Delisle, Saskatchewan, voted "Best Conservative Blog for 2008, combines her rants with feature headlines such as: "Send them Back," "A Perfect Iranian Storm," "Scratch a Leftist, find an Anti-semite," "This Is My Brother Mohammed, And This Is My Other Brother Mohammed." *Blogging Tories*, linked to the Manning Centre for Building Democracy, headed by Preston Manning, is an umbrella site that hosts more than 300 blogs and connections to the Canadian Taxpayers Association, National Citizen's Coalition, etc. The blog features an image of Stephen Harper, in thumbs-up pose, above a counter for the number of days he's been prime minister. Steve Janke's *Angry in the Great White North* picks up the current anger-as-politics rhetoric from the U.S. Tea Party and tries to apply it in Canada. Ezra Levant, a libertarian and the author of *Ethical Oil*, can also boast a significant following. Levant leads the conservative attack against the Human Rights Commission of Canada and all the provincial commissions while he's at it. Levant's voice will become louder from his new perch as a host on Sun TV.

Participant Blogs

Participant blogs are written by journalists or others without training who comment, interview, gather information, post photos and make links while participating in an event or process. They can adopt either an outsider or insider perspective. A traditional journalist will usually make it clear that their participation does not necessarily include acceptance of the event. Non-journalists more often participate as active insiders, who make their sympathies to the purpose or cause clearly understood. The participant blogs of students involved in CUSO projects overseas exemplify what's possible by insiders. These excellent writings show a thoughtful response to their experiences and surroundings. The blogs of Intercordia, another aid and development organization for young people, founded by Jean Vanier, also work this way. These are written on the spot but with enough time to reflect. In some ways these blogs resemble the old group letter, sent home by a person travelling.

Now that tweets have gained wide acceptance, the fast-developing, live reporting of events gets communicated on Twitter, rather than through blogs. The Twitter reporter seems more like the old telephone correspondent.

Citizen Journalists

Online news sites have not only encouraged more people to get into the act, they have also created the possibility for new types of journalism. This is easiest to find at rabble.ca. The weekly installments for the fall of 2010 included a number of excellent examples: "An Indian summer for the tar sands," by Ben Powless (September 13, 2010); "The hidden costs of Canada's banana market" by Kevin Edmonds (September 14, 2010); "Keepers of the Water: A wake-up call from the North" by Rita Wong (September 8, 2010); and "Newfoundland: Some tourists buy post cards, others buy houses," by Emily Urquhart (August 31, 2010).

Citizen journalism is a difficult term to define specifically. Paul Sullivan, a former editor of Orato.com, says that the idea was to "create a platform for people to bear witness in the first person" because there's a lot of wisdom and knowledge untapped in the traditional media.[9] Jay Rosen, an advocate of the form, provides his own witty definition, stating that citizen journalists are "the people formerly known as the audience."[10] Yet, despite this admirable faith in non-professionals, the vagueness of such definitions could make us wonder who these people are. The category of citizen journalists might include:

- students knowledgeable about an issue or field;
- journalism students;
- academics engaging in journalism;
- freelance, out-of-work, or part-time journalists; and
- knowledgeable people without journalism training but with special connections or insights.

Greenpeace employee Mike Hudema, of Edmonton, reflects another possibility. Mike maintains a formidable output of blogging, short articles and Facebook entries about the tar sands developments and attempts to stop them. He is thus a professional communicator and activist whose point of view would rarely turn up in Alberta's media world. Perhaps it's not surprising that Greenpeace would play a leading role in this type of new media creation and distribution. It's a role they have performed creatively since the 1970s.

Tyrone Nicholas created his popular blog "Wente Watch" in

2004 as an outlet for his anger and frustration over the ill-informed writings of senior *Globe and Mail* columnist Margaret Wente. Nicholas wrote a regular critique of Wente's columns, deconstructing their errors, half-truths and biases, especially her writings on climate change and race. This blogging was far more than contrary opinion; it was backed up by fact-checking, analysis of her rhetoric and the countervailing ideas of experts from the fields in question. Such citizen journalism provides an important counter-point to the dominant media. In the end we must conclude that citizen journalism in Canada remains an activity with great potential but so far with few practitioners and little influence. The technology seems to make it easy. The realities of its economics, skill level and time make it difficult unless we can set up organizations to encourage and sustain it.

Podcasts

A podcast is a form of internet radio available to subscribers. When a podcaster creates and posts a new program, it streams out to all subscribers simultaneously. That makes it different from conventional radio in two ways. First, it doesn't get transmitted via sound waves through the atmosphere, and, second, it is not broadcast for anyone to pick up. You can't stumble onto a podcast in the same way you find stations by scanning the radio dial.

Inexpensive technology makes podcasting popular, and the practice has also gained an audience among left and liberal followers of the news, largely because so much commercial radio remains tightly controlled by a very few companies. Podcasting begs us to ask questions. How much genuine news, as opposed to opinion, music or chat, can you find on podcasts? Will citizen-created podcasting reach the same level of quality as in its written forms? What percentage of podcasters have professional training or elementary skills in creating audio? What sorts of politics has podcasting attracted? In North America and Western Europe, the left seems to have jumped into the act first, but since 2007 dominant media podcasting has expanded enormously, mostly in the form of re-packaged radio and TV current affairs.

Social Media: Broadcast Yourself

YouTube burst into the online world in 2005, launched as a way for anyone to post videos online. To a large extent this ever-expanding site has been dominated by U.S. youth anxious to share in the genre of TV bloopers. Others see it as a way of promoting their lifestyle and have no compunction about allowing millions into their lives — warts, tattoos and all. YouTube's motto, "broadcast yourself," suggests the two contradictory possibilities opened up to users. One emphasizes the democratic ideal that anyone can broadcast and the other encourages a largely self-centred activity. YouTube soon became a source for news, which was quickly recognized by mainstream news agencies and their upstart internet rivals. In 2006 Google purchased the entire operation. U.S. news almost totally dominates on YouTube (e.g., on September 20, 2009, seven of the twelve top news clips focused on the U.S.), but channels from China and Taiwan are growing quickly. Mixed in with the millions of clips — the ridiculous, the absurd, the mindless, the grotesque — are significant pieces of world news, often unavailable elsewhere. This includes the broadcasts of Al-Jazeera, a first for most viewers in the Canada. Politicians, even the federal government itself, now use the service for promoting themselves. Thus like blogging, YouTube freely mixes real news and fake news, commentary and advertising. Often the distinctions get a little murky.

YouTube has expanded the possibilities for news. It has worked, for example, as a site for dissident Iranians, Tibetans and Egyptians, and it allows Canadians of all stripes to report on events, investigate stories, etc. Unfortunately, it remains largely potential in terms of original reporting. If you look, for example, at a category such as "Canadian politics," what you see are TV clips, press conferences, bits from events posted by dueling leftists, liberals and right-wingers — a clip of Harper speaking in Parliament, of Trudeau signing the Charter of Rights, someone's speech at a Conservative Party BBQ in London, Ontario, Gay Pride Day in Moncton, New Brunswick, etc. Mixed in with these are a goodly number of animated or PowerPoint essays, some creative and witty, others crude and rude. What you don't find is original journalism or even basic reporting of newsworthy un-staged events. It seems that if people want to make a political point on YouTube, they can find an existing TV clip and make sure that it gets some attention.

Facebook and Twitter provide users with a means of connecting or staying connected to friends and others far afield. Facebook, in particular, makes it easy to share ideas, campaigns, news and some forms of entertainment. For young people especially, it seems to provide a bridge between personal contacts and the larger world, at a time of life when this is not so easy. Mike Hudema and his 2,900 friends certainly offer that link. Corporate advertisers and public relations people now realize that these forms have become essential means of communication. The left must do likewise.

The Digital Divide

The concept of the digital divide illustrates that some people have access to information, ideas and data, while others do not. Writers often apply this idea very generally across the globe, so that we see the North with high rates of computer and online access and the poor South with low rates. Many surveys show that access to digital information is increasing rapidly in the South. But while this may be true (especially for China, Brazil and India), it ignores the gap between rich and poor.

In Canada and the U.S., governments and many educational agencies claim that most citizens now have computer access. However, access to a computer does not mean computer literacy or even a computer in a home — nor does it consider the age and power of the computers. The statistics include computers available at schools and public libraries, and while these machines are essential to society, they do not provide the kind of ready access that everyone needs. In addition, a more accurate measurement must now look at broadband access.

General statistics about computer use hide large disparities by region and ethnicity, between men and women, the young and the old, the upper class and the underclass. First Nations communities, as mentioned earlier, have major problems getting decent broadband services from technology providers. In 2005 fewer than 50 percent of First Nations in B.C. had internet access, and many didn't even have phone connections.[11] Since then, federal and provincial money has improved the situation. However, as Sue Hanley, coordinator of the First Nations Technology Council, points out, high-speed connections may be even more important to her communities "to make up for the lack or absence of emergency, health, and education services," especially in rural areas of the North. "We're out of sight, out of mind — and we get kept that way," says Brian Beaton, of Sioux Lookout, a First Nations community north of Thunder Bay, Ontario.[12]

A widely quoted study, called *Canada Online!,* compiled by the Canadian Internet Project, unsurprisingly puts a positive spin on the growth in online services. But, a careful reading shows that 46 percent of Canadians have no access to broadband and thus lack the means to fully take part. In addition, those who do have access, in the home, schools and libraries, do not necessarily use it. So, for example, the survey counts household access rather than actual use — in a family of three the young person may use a computer and broadband but the parents may not, but the survey implies that everyone is online.[13] Jacquie McNish, a senior business journalist with the *Globe and Mail* points out another factor: "Drive one hour outside most major Canadian cities and digital highways quickly turn to dirt roads filled with potholes…. Only a minority of… rural residents… actually use high-speed broadband because the services are typically too expensive or undependable."[14]

So, considerations of the digital divide should start with these three questions: How many Canadians have access to up-to-date

---

The Digital Gap

Canadian Internet Users 2007
78 percent have access to the internet
54 percent have access to broadband

Source: *Canadian Internet Report*

---

computers (at home, school and work)? How many Canadians have regular access to broadband? How many Canadians have the time and skills to follow the news online? Finally, I suspect that by this point in the life of computers in society there are few people who will admit they are not online. The example of literacy might remind us that a strong stigma exists for people who can't read, and many people will go to great lengths to cover that up. It's true that a significant group have rejected computers altogether and are proud of it. But many of those without access will not readily admit it.

Online Trends

More online news sites get launched every day. Some offer real alternatives to the dominant media, but many online news, blog and social networking services accelerate some dangerous trends. For example, they encourage immediacy, speed and first impressions as the prevailing news values. In most cases they emphasize breadth at the expense of depth of information. Many accelerate the sound-bite culture — a culture of surface phenomena and amnesia, devoid of context and history. Online news sites push the older news media, particularly twenty-four-hour TV, to follow suit. Online sites also contribute to the blurring of boundaries between news and commerce. Many influential online sites depend on advertising, a dependence that can affect their news values. They set fewer rules than their old media counterparts about conflicts of interest for writers, bloggers or editors. They also have fewer mechanisms for recognizing, labelling or rejecting fake news, or even for spotting errors of fact. In the online world, news creation is the priority; news editing is not.

The same sped-up, online, individualist culture applies to online entertainment as well. Thirty-minute sit-coms with tired plot points and laugh tracks prevail, now joined by short segment reality and variety shows and contests. The smaller, inferior screens of handheld devices also imperil the social experience of entertainment. The smaller the device, the bigger the close-ups and the prevalence of talk over image.

For the dominant media, online advertising has grown rapidly, and some predict that advertising will eventually desert the old media entirely. But in 2009, online sites lagged far behind print in generating revenue. Newspapers and broadcasters simply can't charge as much for online ads. For the cable and broadcasting industries in Canada, digital TV means pay TV. The days of free over-the-air signals have nearly past.

Perhaps, we might conclude, this "new" media differs little from the "old" media of underground newspapers, journals and publishers. Haven't these always worked on the margins as it appears new media are designed to do. Nevertheless, new media technologies make much more information and analysis available and with greater potential influence than any oppositional or alternative views in the past.

Even with the problems we have looked at in this chapter, online news and entertainment show great promise for a world of democratic media. In liberal democracies we now have the ability to select news, information and opinions from an international ocean that is both deep and wide. The fresh sources of online news and entertainment allow us to embark on a surfing safari far beyond our old boundaries.

6. INVESTIGATIVE REPORTING

This chapter reviews investigative journalism, how it's currently practised in Canada, and why we need it.

Many newspaper and TV journalists believe that Canada can boast a lengthy tradition of investigative reporting that has unearthed serious social problems. Occasionally journalists have asked more fundamental questions as well, perhaps especially in Quebec, where the rights of labour and of independence have been openly debated. Investigative journalism probes much deeper than normal reporting and often ends up pointing the finger at wrongdoing. But its specialized nature, its lengthy process and its need to take risks make it an expensive activity, which media corporations don't usually relish. Most journalists in Canada say it is declining but that it is far from dead.

A standard news story is based on allegation and denial. These stories are "quite attractive for newspapers. They enable complaints to be aired while saving time on research and minimizing the risk of a libel action," says David Spark a specialist on the form.[1] An investigative story goes further in order to ascertain the facts and then takes a stand. It is not impartial. For this reason some reporters refer to it as advocacy journalism.

"There is no precise formula" for those methods practised by investigative journalists, states historian Cecil Rosner. "They display a keen sense of outrage…. They question why things have worked the way they traditionally do, and are skeptical of conventional explanations," says Rosner. "They feel a need to hold powerful vested interests to account."[2]

Maxine Ruvinsky, a professor of journalism at the University of Manitoba, believes that such journalism "is supposed to identify culprits, whether these be individuals, or an entire system working under cover of 'normalcy.'" Its work "uncovers patterns, not simply isolated incidents," says Ruvinsky. Investigative reporters are after results which have "impact and effect change–not simply relate the facts."[3] Ruvinsky cautions, however, that investigative journalism in "Canada has neither as long or stellar history… as it has in the United States."[4]

Many reporters shy away from the label "investigative" because it sounds arrogant or it's something that all good reporters do anyway. That's "a crock," says David McKie, one of Canada's leading practitioners. "I used to think that [all journalism is investigative], but… there's a difference between what I do and what someone in daily news does, pure and simple. I mean the kind of information we get, the way we get it, the way we work sources — it's different, it's investigative. There's a methodology to it. We may use the he-said-she-said template as a starting point, but not an end point."[5] Kim Bolan, one of Canada's best journalists, prefers to call her work guerrilla journalism, in order to emphasize that the methods needed are not routine. "You realize you're in a war to get the truth out…. You have to adopt creative tactics — non-traditional tactics and means."[6]

In addition to newspapers big and small, the TV programs *Fifth Estate*, on CBC, *W5*, on CTV, and CBC Radio's *Sunday Morning*, along with a number of earlier programs, have produced valuable work.

Free *The Tar Sands*

Peter Pearson's film *The Tar Sands* became a news story itself. "The story involved negotiations between the big oil companies and governments of Canada, Alberta and Ontario that led to $2 billion of public money being earmarked to develop the Athabaska Tar Sands," said Pearson. "The show featured Kenneth Welsh as the Albertan premier (widely known to be an unflattering portrait of Peter Lougheed) along with Donald Brittain's ubiquitous voice-of-God narration. Some critics hailed *The Tar Sands* (based on a book by Larry Pratt) the year's best TV program. Peter Lougheed wasn't so enthusiastic and launched a lawsuit against the network. CBC president Al Johnson wanted to bury it, but the program aired once." The CBC eventually reached an out-of-court settlement with Lougheed for $250,000 and a public apology. Today, *The Tar Sands* is the only episode in the *For the Record* series not available in the CBC tape archives.

Source: Paul Eichhorn, "Journalistic Dramas: *Tar Sands*," *Take One*, Summer, 1998.

Methods

Canadian investigative journalists use a wide variety of methods. Some specialize in the investigation of records, others rely on inside sources or whistleblowers, and most have worked a particular beat (such as crime, business, politics) for many years. Sometimes, however, beat reporters may get too close to the people and institutions they regularly cover. They may take on the views of the group or fear for their future ability to get inside information if they become too critical. In those cases a feature writer or an outsider may be more effective with an investigation. A classic case of the failure of beat reporters and the success of an outsider was the series written by Paul McKay in 2001 for the *Ottawa Citizen* and *Vancouver Sun* about automobiles and car culture. McKay's twenty-one articles looked at dirty gas supplied by Canada's refiners, the health costs of air pollution due to car emissions, the marketing of gas guzzling SUVs and many other topics. These issues are never touched in the papers' auto sections, which bring in major advertising income.

For all those Canadians concerned about how the police handled demonstrators at the G20 conference in Toronto in 2010, it's useful to look back at an important newspaper series that appeared in 2001, called "Criminalizing Dissent." In this case the reporters, David Pugliese and Jim Bronskill, began by close observation of both events and other media coverage. They had noticed a "heavy-handed increase in security forces at demonstrations…. You'd see a two-paragraph story saying [something like], Mr X arrested in advance of a protest. And no one was actually saying much. That was the other disturbing thing: there wasn't a lot of discussion. It was the typical Canadian attitude: Well, I guess they're troublemakers, so throw away the key, right?"[7]

Eventually their series of articles uncovered the existence of a secret RCMP dirty tricks unit and a broader scheme called the Public Order Program. Unfortunately, despite some squirming within the Liberal Party, which was then in power, the series has not diminished the threat to civil liberties in Canada. In fact, reports Maxine Ruvinsky in 2006, it was revealed that Jim Bronskill had himself been the target of government spying, from the Prime Minister's Office. And, while working on similar stories about the Canadian military, Pugliese was the victim of cyber attacks and an anonymous campaign to discredit him, which was traced back to public affairs officers in the military.

Records

Important stories often emerge because reporters look carefully at written sources. They read long, tedious documents, they dig deeply and carefully analyze what they're looking at. For example, reporters compare what officials say versus what they do. A provincial politician might say: "I've always voted in favour of the clean water legislation," but examination of the record might show that the politician was absent for many of the crucial votes.

Other investigations begin with someone comparing types of documents that don't usually get compared, perhaps local cancer rates and industry documents that show where particular companies have operated in the past. Recovering old, obscure or buried documents can take months, even years, to pry from official sources, even when they are supposed to be available through access to information laws.

Computers have given reporters tools to launch investigations which weren't possible before and have made some investigations easier through their ability to process large amounts of data. David McKie, of CBC Radio in Ottawa, carried out a drugs and workplace safety series that showed what was possible.[8] By unearthing and reporting on data compiled by computer, McKie believes: "That's where the real power comes from.... Because it's un-deniable. What is an institution going to do?... It's their own data.'[9] Computer assisted reporting, says McKie, is "the great equalizer, meaning that you don't have to work for the CBC, etc. You can be doing this from your own desktop, and you could be turning out first-rate work."[10] Above all, good reporters learn not to rely on official sources of so-called communications directors and information officers, hired by governments, politicians and corporations determined to control their message. The government of Prime Minister Harper has taken control of its message to new levels, such that even cabinet ministers do not speak without an official script. Simultaneously, on the fringes of power, the world is full of professional marketers and public relations spin doctors desperate to get noticed by the media, working to get their point of view accepted.

Leads, Tips, Whistleblowers

Many investigative stories begin with a phone call to a reporter by someone with inside information, a grudge or a suggestion to look into a situation. Without that initial call we might never know that a wrongdoing or a bad situation is taking place. This is how the horrendous story of the missing women in Vancouver began. In 1997, "Lindsay Kines, as the police beat reporter at the *Vancouver Sun*, first received a call from a woman concerned about her sister, who had apparently disappeared from the Downtown East Side."[11] It was later confirmed that the woman was only one of many — mostly young and Aboriginal — who had vanished, a reality that was finally admitted by the police and eventually led to the trial and conviction of Robert Picton for mass murder.

Other tips can prove to be dangerous, the result of lies or misinformation. These need to be thoroughly checked by the reporter. The most egregious example in recent years involved the situation of Mahar Arar, the Canadian engineer who was accused of having terrorist links, then was illegally arrested and shipped to Syria where he was tortured. At one point in this nasty saga an Ottawa reporter was anonymously given documents that suggested the RCMP believed Arar to be guilty, or at least suspicious. The "leaked" information was untrue but the reporter had already used it in a story.[12]

Women in the Business

Since the 1960s, Canadian journalists have uncovered major problems in the fields of crime, politics and race, taking on elites and major institutions. In a field formerly dominated by men, women now play a significant role.

Stephen Truscott, a fourteen-year-old, was convicted of murder in 1959 and originally sentenced to hang. What happened next shows two sides of the Canadian media: on the one hand was a tenacious journalist who believed in Truscott's innocence; on the other was a timid and conformist book and magazine industry. Fortunately, Isabel Le Bourdais, a freelance magazine writer, followed up with great research and interview skills and after seven years published *The Trial of Steven Truscott.* Unfortunately, Le Bourdais' manuscript had been rejected by many magazines and five Canadian book companies. It was only after Victor Gollancz, the famed British publisher, brought it out that Canadian media began to take an interest.

Beryl Fox worked at CBC Television's current affairs and documentary units when they carried out important investigations in the 1960s. In 1963 she directed *One More River*, the first sustained look at the U.S. civil rights movement. It is a direct cinema documentary that uses new and innovative techniques to film events, including a powerful speech by Malcolm X, and conduct spontaneous interviews with many activists.

Kim Bolan's newspaper articles and book on the Air India tragedy, in which Sikh extremists killed 329 Canadians, required her full-time dedication for twenty-five years. She received many death threats and was forced to live away from home under security protection. Since the late 1990s, she also worked with others on the story of the murdered women from Vancouver's Downtown East Side. In the latter case, her newspaper stepped forward to carry the investigation partly because the police were incapable (or unwilling) of handling it themselves.[13]

Stevie Cameron laboured doggedly for many years to show the systematic corruption in Brian Mulroney's governments. Although she later fell out with other journalists by cooperating with the RCMP in pursuing the wrongdoers, her work was in the public interest and certainly played a role in bringing down Mulroney's Conservative government.

Anne McIlroy wrote a series on the influence of drug companies on medical research at Canada's universities.[14] She was able to demonstrate that researchers and faculty could lose their jobs or have their career ruined if they raised doubts about drugs manufactured by companies who were large medical school funders, such as Eli Lilly and its drug Prozac. McIlroy needed great patience and time to prove her findings because even the most senior faculty members were afraid to speak out. This was a case where the universities had abdicated their responsibility to assure freedom of speech and opinion. Without news media that is free of corporate interference, such issues would not come to light.[15]

In 2005, Louise Elliot, a CBC Radio journalist, worked to uncover the secret testing of the chemical weapons Agent Orange and Agent Purple in Canada during the 1960s. Her work gives a taste of an investigative reporter's methods plus the hard work and luck needed for this kind of reporting. Elliot recalls how one story came about:

> In the spring of 2005, we received a call from a man named Ken Dobbie. He told me his amazing tale. Dobbie had been sick for 30 years and believed, the cause lay in a summer job, back in 1966, when he was just a teenager clearing brush at Canadian Forces Base, Gagetown, New Brunswick. Dobbie was articulate and his story's details, dates, names, and times added up as I looked into them over the following weeks. He described the blackened trees and bushes where no birds sang. He described burning the branches and inhaling fumes without adequate protection. I had that feeling in the pit of my stomach that I get when I hear an incredible story....
>
> In fact, as I began to dig I discovered more civilian stories like Dobbie's: entire towns and villages said they were affected, along with scores of military personnel. I realized a much bigger story about Base Gagetown had never been told: namely, the US army had sprayed not just Agent Orange, but its more toxic cousin, Agent Purple at CFB Gagetown....
>
> Within a week of the stories airing, the Department of Defence promised a comprehensive fact-finding mission that would open the possibility of civilian compensation. From a research point of view, this story was a classic example where information from people led to documents, which led me back to other people to help decipher the documents. It has taught me to be cautious about stories that people think have already been told. In fact, much of this story had never been told.[16]

What It Requires

Investigative reporting is not for everybody. It requires experience and tenacity, independence and strong interviewing skills. Courage doesn't hurt either, when reporters are faced with hate mail, online slander and, in the case of Kim Bolan, ongoing death threats. Her fellow journalist Tara Singh Hayer, founder of the *Indo-Canadian Times*, was murdered in 1998.

It may not be obvious but many of these investigations are undertaken by several journalists with complementary skills, often working as a team. This shows the importance of institutional support from editors, managers and even owners of news organizations. Investigations always need time, money and often legal clout as well.

Conclusion

Unfortunately, there is fodder a-plenty for alert journalists to pursue government corruption, funding scams and sleazy dealing, and although we need skilled people examining these cases they hardly qualify as earth-shattering news. In fact, many times it is only one person or the party in power that falls — leaving room for their twin to take over.

Investigative reporting has rarely tackled systemic economic problems. For example, white collar crime has not been investigated as thoroughly in Canada as in the U.S., a situation that parallels Canadian legal laxity in dealing with corporate malfeasance. The most glaring example was that of media baron Conrad Black, who was finally brought to earth in the U.S. in 2008, first by shareholders in his media companies and then by federal prosecutors. But Black had been operating in Canada on a grand scale since the 1970s without drawing serious media or legal attention about his business methods. The veteran CBC reporter Neil MacDonald does not hold back in his assessment. "Canadian journalism is far too inclined to genuflect to power….When it comes to challenging conventional wisdom, or better, challenging the motives and practices of business,

Canadian journalists are anemic." For Macdonald, "journalists have far less in common with the poor and disadvantaged, and far more in common with executives and the politically powerful."[17] Another Canadian media celebrity, the sports entrepreneur Alan Eagleson, operated in Canada for twenty years before his white-collar crimes were finally revealed in 1990 — not in Canada but as a result of the dogged work of a New Hampshire sports reporter for a small regional paper. Perhaps Canadian sports reporters were too close to Eagleson, too much in the "rah-rah Canada" bubble to see what was happening.

News media throw around the term investigative reporting rather loosely. For the headline writers at the *Sun* chain of tabloids, every front-page story reveals shocking facts, horrendous scandals and mind-bending rip-offs. Mostly, these are nothing of the kind, simply one-sided opinions. Even prestigious shows like the *Fifth Estate* deal regularly in hyperbole. A spring 2010 story about fighting in NHL hockey relies solely on interviews with hockey insiders. No senior management is questioned. The program opened minor cracks of misgiving among players, and the views of one critical sports journalist were aired. But, in the end the only *Fifth Estate* revelation is that players fight according to a code of honour.

Journalists' self-congratulations need to be tempered with much stronger work. New libel laws should make it easier, said Kathy English of the *Toronto Star* during a Freedom to Read Week panel discussion in Toronto in February 2010. The Supreme Court judgements give journalists more room to defend stories in court using the new argument of "responsible communication on matters of public interest." Let us see what happens now that reporters have been given more freedom.

7. MEDIA AND SOCIETY

CanCon

During the 1960s, a new wave of nationalism swept across the world, especially in Africa, South America and the Caribbean. In Canada, some of this was directed from the top down. Economists, for example, worried about the influence of the U.S., specifically about the takeover of key business sectors. Federalist politicians, such as Pierre Trudeau, panicked about the strong desire for independence taking shape in Quebec. Many ordinary Canadians began to question our culture's dependence on the U.S. and some of its values, particularly the U.S. government's increasingly aggressive foreign policies, for example, in Vietnam and Cuba. A strong peace movement fought against the practice of U.S. weapons testing on Canadian soil. Teachers and parents became increasingly disturbed that U.S. cultural values were being shoved down the throats of Canadian young people.

For these and other reasons, the federal government launched major initiatives to foster Canadian content in the arts and education. These policy initiatives serve as clear examples of the Canadian government and its agencies using media to influence society at a deep level. Every such policy the federal government created rested on two underlying goals — to hold back the tide of U.S. cultural influence and to counter demands for Quebec independence. It was only much later that federal planners realized the economic benefits of these programs. Healthy media create jobs and stimulate Canadian-based technology. In music, book and magazine publishing, and children's TV, the efforts to create Canadian content, CanCon, met with particular success.

Music

In 1971, the government, through the CRTC, insisted that radio stations play at least 30 percent Canadian music. The private broadcasters lobbied hard against this, saying that listeners only wanted the best and there was little appetite for Canadian music. Let the CBC take care of that, they argued. Yet, within ten years, a flood of Canadian popular music filled the airwaves and had made a significant impact in the U.S. as well. This also created a Canadian star system, complete with fan magazine and advertising support. Most musicians would agree that the 30 percent policy had been essential. In 1998, the percentage was raised to 35 percent with a lot less fuss.

Book Publishing

In 1970, Canada's oldest publisher, Ryerson Press, was sold to the U.S. giant McGraw-Hill. Ryerson had built a reputation for supporting Canadian literature and was a major school text producer. The sale created panic in educational circles and in Ottawa. Consequently, within a year the government had bailed out a number of publishers and set up an ongoing grant program to insure that Canadian textbooks in particular not be dominated by U.S. content. This new support system lit the fuse for significant movements in Canadian fiction, nonfiction and children's literature. It was a dramatic expansion of Canadian publishing: the Independent Publishers Association started in 1971 with sixteen members; in 2011, its successor group, the Association of Canadian Publishers, boasts more than 150. In the 1970s, the economy was still healthy enough to provide adequate funding for educational spending in most provinces, so schools and libraries had plenty of money to purchase Canadian material of all kinds.[1]

Children's TV

The development of Canadian children's TV was not influenced as directly by the cultural scare of the early 1970s. For one thing, the CBC/Radio Canada already boasted a steady record of popular children's shows, some of which stretched back to the 1950s. However, by the 1980s, the rise of children's book and magazine publishing had created a solid new base for film and TV programs to draw on. Another key incentive was the U.S. program *Sesame Street* (1969–), which provided a new model for educational TV — a model wildly successful in affecting children's culture in general. Also, the economy in the 1970s had cut the standard of living for most working Canadians and forced many women to rejoin the workforce. Simultaneously, a new baby boom, later dubbed Generation X, was emerging. Both these factors helped put TV in the centre of most homes and created the demand and market for CanCon TV. One success story was the publisher KidsCan Press, started in 1973, which developed Franklin the Turtle, among many other characters, and then joined up with the animation company Nelvana to produce children's shows. Other successful ventures emerged from new provincial educational broadcasters, especially TVOntario and Radio Quebec (now Tele-Quebec). Partly stimulated by *Sesame Street,* these pioneered new types of TV for children, using animation, puppets and above all Canadian references.

Children's television in Canada has a long history of providing a gentler alternative to some of the over-the-top programs being shown elsewhere. Classic programs like *Mr. Dressup* and *The Friendly Giant* allowed children to indulge in a more interactive experience with program hosts, who made a personal connection with their young viewers.[2]

Canuck Kids TV Hits

Maggie Muggins (1955 –1962) CBC
Jake and the Kid (1961–1963) CBC
Razzle Dazzle (1961–1966) CBC, featuring Michele Finney and
Howard the Turtle
The Friendly Giant (1958–1985) CBC, featuring Bob Homme in
3,000 episodes
Mr. Dressup (1967–1996) CBC, featuring Ernie Coombs
Passe-partout (1977–87) Radio-Quebec
Degrassi Jr. High (1987–1989) CBC (followed by *The Kids of
Degrassi Street*, *Degrassi High*, and *Degrassi: The Next Generation*)
The Adventures of Dudley the Dragon (1993–1997) YTV
Theodore Tugboat (1993–1998) shot in Halifax for the CBC
Caillou (1998–2006) Radio Canada
Watatatow (1991–2005) Radio Canada — one of the most success-
ful shows ever in Canada — 1,220 episodes.

Film historian Blain Allan tells the story of one early children's drama series:

> *Radisson* (1957–1958) was the first major dramatic series produced on film in Canada. Radisson attracted inevitable comparisons with Walt Disney's Davy Crockett films, phenomenally popular in the U.S.A. and Canada when they were first broadcast in 1955. In fact, the serialized adventures of explorer Pierre Esprit Radisson were generally thought a response to the Disney series, with all the attendant merchandising and publicity.
>
> The idea for the series belonged to Monica Clare, the CBC's national organizer of children's programming…. The adventures of Radisson had also arisen as a prospect in the French language division of the CBC, and plans went ahead to produce a series with one cast in both French and English, as the network was doing with the live, studio production, *The Plouffe Family*.

Early on, Jacques Godin, a twenty-six year old actor with the Theatre du Nouveau Monde, was cast as Radisson. Subsequently René Caron signed to play Groseilliers, Radisson's sidekick. The series was shot in Montreal studios and at Ile Perrot, on the St. Lawrence River southwest of Montreal....

Shooting started on 20 August 1956, with a scheduled television premiere two months later. The budget was originally set at $7,000 per episode, but shortly had to be raised to $15,000, and the targeted premiere had to be pushed back to December. The production was plagued with problems: swarms of mosquitoes, St. Lawrence river traffic that upset the already unsteady birchbark canoes, airplanes from Dorval airport and trains that regularly disrupted the authenticity of the seventeenth century period piece, and especially weather, which stalled production for twenty-three days out of the first month and a half. As time wore on and winter approached, the costs escalated to an estimated $25,000 per episode.

When the series finally appeared on television sets in French on 3 February 1957 and in English the following Friday, the 8th, the CBC hoped that the adventures of Radisson would capture Canadians' attention and imagination, and advertisers, merchandisers, and John Lucarotti, who licensed the television character, hoped that those viewers would snap up Radisson gear the way they had swallowed the Davy Crockett image.

The battle for kid's eyes and brains continues, with such U.S. networks as Disney and Nickelodeon a strong presence in Canada.

Mirrors and Impacts

Media influence other media, media reflect society, and media affect society. In the discussions below, keep in mind that all three types of relation can work simultaneously.

Media Influence Media

All media forms are created from the genres and conventions that went before. No media form, no matter how closely it appears to flow directly from society, stands entirely on its own. There are always as many allusions to other media forms in any single text as reflections of the outside world. Even the most factually based newscast uses the conventions of newscasts as a genre.

When Colm Feore, as a straight-laced Toronto detective, joins Patrick Huard, his corrupt but loveable counterpart from Montreal, in *Bon Cop Bad Cop* (Eric Canuel, 2006), we witness only the latest in a long line of mis-matched buddy cops, stretching back to those multi-racial couples Mel Gibson and Danny Glover, Rod Steiger and Sidney Poitier, and Jackie Chan and Chris Carter. Even when the society is changing, the media often don't reflect those changes because the forms and genres of media exert an even stronger influence. For example, while women are making gains in some occupations, the genre of male buddy films remains strong.

Media Reflect Society

The best way to know what's going on in any society, many people believe, is to study its popular media. Accordingly, social trends, general fears and aspirations, the status of various groups and the power of ruling elites are often reflected in the media. When you hear people talking about media as a mirror of society, they are framing their comments in this context. One way of thinking about these issues is to compare similar media forms created in different countries or regions of the world. The family melodrama, for example, contains similarities across the world, but, as we saw earlier, Quebec's *téléroman*, such as *Les Plouffe*, differs significantly from the U.S. soap opera. The depiction of social class in the Québécois fiction certainly reflects this as a vital issue in Quebec society.

Yet, as many have observed, the media's mirror usually works more like a fun-house distorting mirror. And as mentioned above, media are often slow to recognize changes in society. They do, however, reflect a society's power dynamics, and they don't simply reflect; they provide the symbols, images, ideas and frames that constitute power itself. In other words, the dominant media create some of the forms by which power operates. The CBC's mini-series *Trudeau*, from 2002, two years after his death, provided a symbolic frame to view his life, particularly for younger viewers, as a tough champion for Canadian federalism. In addition to the symbolic, the media industries now constitute power centres themselves (along with courts, schools, churches and police) due to their economic clout and central role in communications.

The Italian Marxist Antonio Gramsci developed the concept of hegemony to explain how power is wielded in the modern state. Hegemony is a form of rule where the elite maintain their position through the creation of a particular worldview, one that seems to be based on common sense. Hegemony doesn't confine itself to intellectual ideas but works within everyday culture and seems to provide a frame for understanding experience. The various media forms, from the newscast to the blockbuster, don't simply communicate hegemonic ideas that have been created in the boardrooms and halls of power, they represent those ideas and ways of thinking in specific media forms. Society's power holders construct a dominant ideology or way of thinking and viewing the world. This force operates only when these ideas can be represented and communicated. The media are not separate from society; the media are part of it.

Ed Herman and Noam Chomsky's propaganda model in their book *Manufacturing Consent* develops the idea that hegemony is a form of rule that requires the consent of citizens.[3] This consent gets manufactured partially through a filtering process in the news media. They suggest five types of filters:

1st Filter — Business Interests of Owners

Favourable coverage / no coverage

2nd Filter — Selling Audiences to Advertisers

Take a look in your newspaper's automotive section. You'll see quickly that car companies take out big ads. Really big full-page ads. In the *Toronto Star*, for instance, it can be hard to find the "news" articles for all the ads. Is it any surprise that few journalists question the decisions being made in Canada's car companies?

3rd Filter — Sourcing Information from Agents of Power

The most cited economic experts in the Canadian media, including by the CBC, are from right-wing think-tanks such as the Fraser and the C.D. Howe Institutes. Jean Swanson, in her book *Poor Bashing*,[4] has traced how the frameworks, concepts and language from these institutes finds its way into the dominant media.

4th Filter — Flak, Pressure on Journalists and Threats of Legal Action

In 2009, two significant legal cases were initiated by Canadian corporations. In one, Barrick Gold threatened to sue the tiny Quebec publisher Les Editions Ecosociete Inc. for $6 million if they published a book critical of Barrick's operations in Africa. The publisher faced bankruptcy if it tried to fight. And in British Columbia, CanWest Global took two artists and several Palestinian rights supporters to court over a political satire of the *Vancouver Sun*'s pro-Israel coverage.

5th Filter — Ideological Beliefs of Journalists

Other sorts of pressures and built-in structures affect how news gets reported and shaped. Racism in the news media, for example, often emerges as a result of social attitudes and pressures on journalists. Several British studies, which also apply here, have highlighted reasons why racist stories appear. These include journalist's and media owners' personal prejudices; the ethnic composition (overwhelmingly white) in the newsroom; inadequate training of journalists; marketplace pressures to serve the maximum number of readers, which in Canada means the white majority; bureaucratic inertia in seeking out diverse news sources; and deep-seated news values that focus on conflict, violence, controversy and deviance.

6th Filter — Political Interests of Owners

Another filter, not mentioned by Herman and Chomsky, involves the political goals and preferences of media owners. For example, the CanWest newspapers, under the Asper family, and *La Presse*, under the Desmarais in Quebec, were clearly linked to the federal Liberal Party. Heather Reisman, CEO of the Chapters/Indigo book chain, and her husband Gerry Schwartz, who has played a major role in Cineplex movie theatres, use their influence openly to lobby for the State of Israel.

Media Affect Society

While theories as to how the media reflect the larger society provide us with valuable kinds of understanding, it's the debates over media influence that generate the most heat and controversy. Thus, the third customary way of talking about the media is to express concern or admiration over its effects. This discourse of media effects has a long history, beginning in its modern form with the birth of cinema in the 1890s and its possible role in corrupting the morals of youth. Do the following types of statements sound familiar? Many people firmly believe them; most remain difficult to prove.

Fashion — everyone's wearing those black Avril Lavigne mini-skirts.

Manners — vulgarity in music lyrics leads to increasing vulgar speech among youth.

Fears — excessive violence on TV screens causes teenagers to become violent.

Behaviour — positive images of men as fathers influence real fathers to take more responsibility.

Knowledge — hearing traditional music on CDs leads to a rediscovery of the old forms and a greater respect for one's culture.

Aspirations — when young people from Canada's First Nations see depictions of southern lifestyles they become restless and demand change.

Crime — U.S.-style gangsta rap glorifies gangs and leads to more crime with guns in Canada.

Discontent — newspaper series on corruption in the provincial government causes voters to kick them out on election day.

Let's move deeper into the arguments about media impact and begin by dividing media effects into three categories: long, medium and short range. Long-range media effects shape us as a species or in our overall organization of society. Medium-range effects influence us as members of social groups. Short-range effects work on a smaller scale, perhaps influencing our personal lives. The following are some typical statements about media effects:

Large-Scale Media Effects

Negative. Media saturation works as an opiate, dulling our senses, making us jaded about the real world. The American Academy of Pediatrics states that children under two-years old should not watch television, saying that TV can hinder proper brain development.

Positive. Cheap and accessible media such as radio, recording machines and handheld devices stimulate better communication and new forms of cultural expression.

Medium-Scale Media Effects

Negative. Media play a key role in racial, ethnic and gender stereotyping, leading to increased tension and misunderstanding about other groups in society. The Vancouver anti-poverty activist Jean Swanson refers to the media depiction of poor people as "poornography."[3]

Positive. Media introduces us to people and places and regions across Canada that we would never be able to visit — thus breaking down barriers to better understanding and bringing Canada into the global age. The dominant media made repeated, nearly ecstatic, claims about the positive role of the Vancouver Olympics in 2010

— "Don't worry about the cost, they implied, the games brought us together as a country."

Small-Scale Media Effects

Negative. The proliferation of media and the voracious appetite of media channels for "product" leads to a standardization of ideas and cultural forms and to such rapid turnover that style and novelty and "the latest thing" become ends in themselves.

Positive. "Let a hundred flowers bloom," said Mao. The growth of media forms and channels fosters rich possibilities for many styles and approaches for art, education and political communication. The globalization of culture makes it possible to draw on artistic talent from anywhere.

Media Effects: Violence

Violence ranks as the number one controversy in discussions about the effect of the media. From the new mass circulation newspapers of the late nineteenth century, and from early cinema's fascination with the chase, crime and criminals, to today's steady diet of murder and mayhem, critics of the media have stated over and over that film, TV and popular music contain too much violence. Social critics, religious groups and governments often chime in. An oft-quoted statistic is that the average U.S. child watching TV three hours a day has by grade seven witnessed 8,000 murders and more than 100,000 other acts of violence. From the local newscast, to reality cops, to crime dramas, to children's animation, violence functions as the central dramatic tool in telling stories and packaging the news.

Many researchers claim that repeated exposure to violence causes not only short- and medium-term damage but also fosters long-range effects on the entire society. Some argue that exposure has both general effects, such as a jaded view of the world and the tendency to objectify others, and specific effects, such as the belief that the world is a more, or less, dangerous place than is really the case.

Unfortunately, the debates over violence have been rife with unsubstantiated claims, half-baked theories, biased opinions and potent doses of fear. Myths and misconceptions litter the ground. Critics of research into the effects of media violence attack the faults of and biases behind the studies. Jonathan Freedman, a University of Toronto media analyst, writes that virtually all the violent-effects studies contain serious flaws. He claims that many of the studies actually show that violent images have no effects but that the researchers are too blind or biased to admit it.[5] Other theorists point to the hidden agendas of some researchers, labelling them witch-hunters and moralists. They remind us that much of the early effects research began in the public relations and advertising worlds of the 1950s, where media effects were taken for granted and where the goal was to understand behaviour triggers in order to sell people more products.

Unfortunately, the no-effects approach remains largely reactive and can point to few studies to back up its position. Thus we should ask: "Do weak proofs and flawed studies mean that violent media produce no effects?"

No matter what the approach, those critics and concerned media watchers who take up the issues of media violence almost always mix their concerns with other agendas. When you hear talk about violence in the media, "There's usually something at stake, politically speaking, in choosing to adopt one stance over another," say Cynthia Carter and Kay Weaver, writing on the politics of the violence debates.[6]

A rough way of categorizing people who take part in debates on the effects of violence in media is to divide them into maximizers and minimizers. The maximizers include the following:

- religious groups which see violence in media as a symbol of declining morals and social decay. These concerns cross many religious paths throughout the world. The religious right in the Canada use campaigns against media violence to attack permissive values onscreen and in schools;

- governments who hop on the maximizers' bandwagon, either from a concern that too much media violence could undermine public order or as a handy tool to gain voter attention;
- the advertising industry, which certainly believes in media effects (that's what they base their sales pitches on);
- nationalists of many kinds, who point to the U.S. entertainment industry's addiction to violence. In Quebec, some social critics worry about the violence in Quebec feature films; and
- a wide spectrum of left and liberal social critics who base their critique of commercial culture on violence in the media. Feminists and anti-racism organizations consistently argue that violence toward them in media representations fosters negative behavioural, desensitizing or cultivation effects. Groups in this category include Media Watch, the Chinese Canadian National Council and the National Anti-Poverty Organization.

The minimizers are found in varied groups as well:

- the entertainment industry, in Canada and the U.S., from film producers to video game manufacturers, officially expresses concern over troubling social issues, including crime. When pushed to the wall, however, they argue vigorously that their products cause no negative effects;
- anti-censorship groups, usually led by those with the most liberal or right-wing libertarian attitudes, downplay connections between media violence and real violence. Their fear, unfortunately too often justified, is that the state or religious groups will use theories of media violence to limit free expression, minority opinion and political dissent; and
- some social and political critics on the left dismiss the entire concern over media effects. They argue that capitalism's structural problems of poverty, racism and unemployment pose far greater threats: these are the real causes of crime. Media, they argue, just provide an easy 'target and a distraction from the real issues.

Violence and War: The Missing Red

Ironically, although we are exposed to a tremendous amount of violence in Western entertainment and domestic news coverage, the opposite is true in representations of war and international conflict. Coverage of war is sanitized, largely cut off from the violence and trauma, especially wars where "we" have a stake.

One conflict where Canada has played a significant role is in Haiti. This long and complex story stretches back at least as far as the horrific dictatorships of Papa Doc and Baby Doc Duvalier during the years 1957–1986. Canadian banks and corporations have operated for many years in the country. These include Gildan textiles and Lavelin of Montreal, as well as several mining companies — 176 companies in all. Canada has played a major role in the country, sending troops, military and RCMP trainers, NGOs and religious leaders. And yet, when the massive earthquake hit Haiti in 2010, we were reminded that Haiti remains the poorest country in the Western world, one of the poorest on earth. Where was the background information on Canada's ongoing role? If Canada has been so involved, do we also take responsibility for the horrendous living conditions of the majority of Haiti's citizens?[7]

A Canadian police expert asked the same question in 2004: "A commander of the UN Civilian Police Unit from Quebec City declared that he is 'in shock' with the conditions he faces in Port-au-Prince. He said his UN mandate is to '(i) coach, (ii) train, and (iii) provide information,' but that all he has done in Haiti is 'engage in daily guerrilla warfare.' As semi-automatic gunfire peppered the interview outside the Church of Our Lady of Perpetual Help in Bel Air, he asked, 'where are the newspaper reporters?'"[8]

Yves Engler, author of *The Black Book of Canadian Foreign Policy* (2009) and *Canada in Haiti* (2005), believes that "our tax dollars have been spent to overthrow a fledgling democracy and to promote an illegal government that engages in massive human rights abuses." In January 2003, the Canadian government organized what it called the "Ottawa Initiative on Haiti," involving the U.S., France and others. One year later, on February 29, 2004, Haiti experienced a coup d'état.

Shortly after the January 2010 earthquake, the media did report endlessly on government and bank promises of $5.3 billion for Haiti's reconstruction. However, according to one calculation, less than 10 percent of those promises had been delivered six months later. To my knowledge this has not been reported here.[9] When it comes to Western war reporting, Gramsci's notion of hegemony seems too subtle. What we usually experience is a closing of media ranks behind "our" government and "our" boys. The propaganda machine seems like a better description. In Canada, the fighting in Afghanistan by Canadian troops always gets framed as "the Mission." In Haiti, it's police training.

In 2006, *Globe and Mail* TV critic John Doyle took on the most public figure in Canadian media, Peter Mansbridge, over the CBC's handling of the conflict in Afghanistan. Doyle charged that the CBC's "obsession with the military" felt "creepy." This was a rare occurrence in the dominant media and a sign of tensions within Canada's elites about how to handle the war.

> The other night, I turned on *The National* on CBC, expecting the day's news coverage, as any person might. Up popped Pastor Mansbridge in a black turtleneck sweater and suede jacket, yakking at me from a military base near Edmonton. He informed viewers that this special edition of *The National* was about "the home front" or some equally inane phrase. It was about our military and the mission in Afghanistan, in other words. But it was couched in we're-all-in-this-together coverage of the military and their families in that Edmonton location.
>
> There was an air of giddiness and excitement. The CBC's obsession with the military bespeaks a diminution of journalistic standards that is reprehensible at any time, but

the clear and obvious linking of the military with the holiday season is simply appalling. It sentimentalizes the armed forces and their action in Afghanistan. War is not something to be sentimentalized at any time. To sentimentalize is to fetishize under the guise of good feeling. To fetishize the military is to appeal to the authorities for respect. And in this case, "authority" is the minority Conservative government.[10]

"We have no apologies to make," replied Mansbridge.[11]

In this chapter I talk about how media affect society and conversely how society affects media. For many issues, the debates centre on what's doing the influencing and what's being affected. For example, many people say that the internet with its constant flow of information, is causing us to have a shorter attention span. Others say that the internet merely reflects the changes that have been taking place in our work, cities and family lives. Thousands of people have two jobs and many responsibilities — thousands of families are spread across the country — everyone is stretched for time. The internet and mobile devices for phone and text, information and entertainment, simply address the needs of our lives. Television, the internet and gaming are drawing more and more flak in connection with children's health. We're facing an obesity epidemic, say the lifestyle columnists in the newspapers: "Kids no longer want to play outside, discover the city or rural byways. They don't read much; they're only interested in looking at screens." The media culprits are pretty easy to discern. In Canada, unlike the U.S., these health concerns may soon out-number worries about violence and media use.

Recommendations

Canada's dominant media serve the interests primarily of their owners and the elites in government and corporations. Until that changes we won't have a democratic media. This chapter contains several proposals, many that have been made before, that could prepare the way for a better media world. The fact that some have been attacked or ignored in the past does not rule out their value today.

Entertainment

- Return to decent levels of drama funding at CBC television so that prime-time is filled with Canadian high-quality productions. Give the CBC its independence by providing stable, multi-year funding.
- Facilitate French/English co-productions through financial incentives, such as tax breaks, municipal sharing of facilities and a separate marketing fund.
- Insist, through political lobbying and the mechanisms of the CRTC, that entertainment broadcasters reflect the diversity of Canada's population. Facilitate a more accurate representation of the multi-racial, multi-ethnic reality of Canada.
- Re-package the best of the CBC for broadcast on the CBC and elsewhere, including shows from the 1950s to the present.
- Create new distribution and exhibition policies to get Canadian films into theatres. Prepare for the backlash from Hollywood and the U.S. State Department.
- Invite initiatives to develop a Canadian star system — as in Quebec — through funding for magazines, TV and radio programs, in-theatre shorts, etc.
- Support independent radio drama through federal and provincial funding.
- Initiate new levels of provincial support for media studies programs and curricula in secondary and post-secondary institutions.
- Require cable and satellite services to prioritize Canadian stations; move the Aboriginal Peoples TV Network onto basic cable.
- Declare a moratorium on cop shows. Let's make a clean break from the Americans and the Brits. Let's show that drama, suspense, workplace conflict, good and bad people, right and wrong, mystery, skill and heroism do not always involve police.

News

Citizen's groups, political organizations, unions, churches, NGOs, etc. must step up their lobbying efforts in order to:

- Stop the phase-out of free, over-the-air television, planned for 2012. At least 10 percent of Canadians will be affected.[12]
- Make investigative reporting a high priority for all news media, unfettered by commercial or political influences.
- Insist that the dominant media report on and thoroughly investigate the tar sands, the activities of the Canadian military, especially in Afghanistan, and the realities of climate change.
- Make the concentration and quality of our news media a political issue.
- Challenge the federal government's suppression of information.
- Re-affirm the principle of the separation of church and state in Canadian broadcasting — insist that religious broadcasting be non-denominational.
- Insist, through political lobbying and the mechanisms of the CRTC, that news organizations reflect the diversity of Canada's population. This must be at all levels, from reporters to senior management.
- Support independent media to cover those issues ignored by the dominant media, through major campaigns by labour and NGOs.
- Establish a labour-based radio network for news and critical analysis of the dominant media.
- Independent media (magazines, community radio and online sites) must start to report on the dominant media *seriously* and hold journalists to a higher standard.

Break Up the Monopolies

Way back in 1981 the Royal Commission on Newspapers, chaired by Tom Kent, proposed "a set of dramatic recommendations."[13] These included:

- limits on the size of the largest newspaper monopolies (of particular concern the Irving monopoly in New Brunswick);
- limits on cross-media ownership, for example, restricting the ownership of a TV station and newspaper in the same city;
- tax incentives to newspapers that print more than the average news and editorial content; and
- require newspapers to write a public statement about their principles and purpose, which would be audited yearly, in order to lift the lid on newspapers' editorial secrecy or hidden agendas.

The negative reaction to the Kent Commission from business in general and newspapers in particular was fierce. Some of the comments included phrases such as idiot's delight, monstrous, vindictive, unacceptable and dangerous. "Reads a bit like a psychedelic dream," said the *Saskatoon Leader-Post*. In the end, the Trudeau government did limit some forms of cross-media ownership, but these changes were quickly overturned when the Mulroney Conservatives came to power in 1984. All the other ideas were rejected.

Since the 1990s, the nature and scope of telecommunications has become obvious to more citizens. The federal government needs to re-commit to its investment in the infrastructure needed for all the forms of digital media. It also needs to insist to the cable and telecommunications corporations that universal access remains a top priority. They too must invest in the required structures — rural and less populated regions must be guaranteed cheap and reliable broadband. Canadian spending in this area should at least match that of the smaller European nations.

Sun TV: The Saga Continues

Three months after Kory Teneycke bounded onto the Sun TV stage for his grand announcement he abruptly quit. He clearly relished his role as a leading conservative pitchman. Now, he says, he just wants to be left alone to "lick my wounds for a while."[18]

A few weeks after the May 2010 launch, a fast-moving internet and letter-writing campaign made the news, with thousands of Canadians stating that the last thing they needed was extremist right-wingers shouting over our airwaves.

More weeks went by and it was revealed that the prime minister's office may have been trying to influence the CRTC into giving a special licence to Sun TV that would put them on basic cable services — a process not currently allowed. It looked as if the PMO might be trying to weaken or circumvent the CRTC.

A few weeks later, Linda McQuaig, writing in the *Toronto Star*, revealed that Prime Minister Harper had met in New York with media boss Rupert Murdoch, the owner of Fox TV. Perhaps Murdoch would be assisted in moving into Canada, somehow flaunting the current regulations against foreign TV.

Teneycke's resignation in September came "a day after a group called Avaaz sent letters to the RCMP and Ottawa police asking them to launch criminal investigations into the adding of 'fraudulent' signatures to the organization's 'Stop Fox News North' petition."

In January 2011, Teneycke re-appeared once more at Sun Media as vice-president of news. But it wasn't long before Mr. Teneycke fumbled again and made himself part of another story. In March, during the federal elections, Sun newspapers printed a photo that supposedly showed Michael Ignatieff proudly holding a rifle in Afghanistan just weeks before the U.S. invasion, in 2003. Soon after, it became clear that the photo had either been doctored or had depicted an Ignatieff look-alike. Subsequently, Sun's president and CEO, Peladeau, was forced to write a lengthy explanation, blaming not Teneycke for sloppiness or fakery but the standard "cut and thrust of any election campaign."[19]

Sun TV News thus marches onward, playing the awkward role of right-wing outsiders while their soulmates run the country via the new Conservative majority. As many people predicted, the network runs almost no news, which they have undoubtedly found expensive to gather and rather complex in its details. Opinion, rants and raised-voice indignation dominate the air. Thus, CBC and CTV remain Canada's dominant news broadcasters. They have nothing to fear from Sun.

APPENDIX

Canada's Dominant Media: Institutions and Structures

Throughout the book I use the concept of dominant media to refer to the group of big companies, institutions and organizations of the so-called mass media. The term "dominant" reminds us that these groups are not only big financially but politically powerful as well. They help set the rules for all media in Canada and have the power to push smaller or more disruptive groups to the sidelines. The group includes both commercial media companies and government organizations. This classic concept of dominant media in Canada stretches back to the foundational works of John Porter in *The Vertical Mosaic* (1965), Wallace Clement in *The Canadian Corporate Elite* (1975), and even in the Canadian Senate's *Report on the Mass Media* of 1970.

As of 2011 the following groups comprise Canada's dominant media:

* CBC / Radio Canada — Canadian Broadcasting Corporation / Radio Canada
* BCE Inc. (Bell Canada, CTV Network, etc.)
* *Globe and Mail*
* Postmedia Network
* Shaw Communications Inc.

- Rogers Communications Inc.
- Quebecor Inc.
- Corus Entertainment Inc.
- Irving Group
- CRTC — Canadian Radio-television and Telecommunications Commission

When analyzing the media, it is useful to talk about institutions, a term that carries two meanings. An institution can be defined as *an organization* founded and united for a specific purpose, such as the CRTC, or as *a custom* that has long been an important feature of some group or society, such as "the institution of journalism." In both meanings an institution can bring pressure to bear on the production and delivery of news and entertainment.

The concept of "structure" is also useful. Thus we can say that corporations, or institutions, or customs have an internal structure. We speak of the structure of a hand and the structure of a skyscraper; in the same way we can speak of the structure of a newspaper. Structure can't always be seen — we have to get below the surface — sometimes to dig very deeply to understand how something works (or why something works the way it does).

Both institutions and structures have histories; they are always changing — in ways we can see and in other ways that we can't. Inside can be churning, while outside all is tranquility.

Canadian Broadcasting Corporation / Radio Canada

At the centre of Canada's media universe sits the CBC, its sister French service, Radio Canada, and its Northern Service. The national radio network was born in 1936, after many years of experiments, controversies and competing ideas. The television service began broadcasting in 1952.

As we have seen, the CBC is the product of many forces — nationalism, the needs of the Canadian state, class dynamics and the desire for media to serve the public, not simply the government or private interests. These forces are just as active today as in the 1930s. What we have, therefore, is a little of everything. Although supposedly an independent institution, at "arm's length" from the government, the corporation only receives funding on a yearly basis. Therefore, the government of the day can continually exert its influence. Yearly funding is approximately $1 billion. This may seem like a lot but it falls far short of what's required, so that for the TV operations the corporation must raise significant money through advertising. One reason why CBC Radio maintains a more loyal audience is undoubtedly because it contains no ads.

In many ways the CBC is the most sophisticated institution within Canadian society. It must serve a very broad and diverse public, and it provides the most symbolic glue in maintaining the unity of the country. Darryl Varga refers to the CBC as a "peacemaker," as the military also likes to define itself.[1] Not only does the government expect the CBC to communicate its policies and play a key symbolic role, but most Canadians expect the highest standards of journalism and entertainment from "their" national broadcaster. That includes playing journalism's roles of investigation, analysis and uncovering wrongdoing, even in government. Canada's newspapers and other media are not expected to play all these roles.

Within the institution of the CBC we can find bureaucrats who answer only to the federal government, senior producers and managers who believe in Canadian nationalism above all else, and producers, editors, creators, etc. who see journalistic principles as their highest goal, regardless of the consequences. For this reason it is difficult to generalize about the functions of the CBC in Canadian society. At one moment it serves as the mouthpiece of the state; at another it uncovers serious crimes and misdemeanors among the country's elites. At one moment it produces serious and popular drama to rank with anything at the BBC; at other moments it spits out appalling drek that reflects well on no-one. It's an institution that pays big salaries to both Lyndon McIntyre, one of the country's best investigative reporters, and Don Cherry, the voice of hockey violence and jingoism.

BCE Inc.

BCE is Canada's largest and oldest communications company. It is the parent of Bell Canada Telecommunications and the CTV television network. The Bell Telephone Company of Canada dates further back than any other entity in this list. BCE is much larger and wider than telephones. Its control of the CTV network puts it at the centre of Canadian media. In addition, its history and continuing power make it an essential service in communications and one of the major companies of Canadian capitalism. Bell no longer operates as a monopoly because Canada's national phone system was opened to private entities in the 1980s. However, it operates now as an oligopoly along with Telus and Rogers.

Globe and Mail

The *Globe and Mail* has served since the 1950s as the country's newspaper for the elites and their first source of information. It is now controlled financially by Thomson Reuters, one of the largest media companies in the world and a third-generation newspaper dynasty. The editorial board of the *Globe* and its leading political and business writers maintain considerable influence over the federal government, as shown in the story about of Paul Martin.

Paul Martin Visits the *Globe and Mail*

In 1994, the Liberal Finance Minister Paul Martin announced his first series of budget cuts, including a deep attack into Unemployment Insurance. Linda McQuaig describes what happened when Martin came to sell his ideas to the editors at the *Globe and Mail*. Martin's ideas were "clearly anathema to senior *Globe* editors," says McQuaig. "What is striking about Martin's meeting… was how single-minded the *Globe* side was…. One is struck by how all the *Globe* editors, reporters and columnists who spoke… shared a single point of view. They accused Martin of not cutting the deficit deeply enough."

Source: Linda McQuaig, *The Cult of Impotence: Selling the Myth of Powerlessness in the Global Economy* (Toronto: Penguin, 1998), pp. 88–89.

Postmedia Network Inc.

Outside Toronto and Montreal, Canadians have very little choice in newspapers. That's because for countless years one chain or another has owned nearly all of them. For many years, it was Southam, then

Conrad Black's Hollinger, then CanWest, and since 2010, Postmedia. The board of directors for Postmedia illustrates the close links between Canada's media and other major corporations. For example, the chair, Ron Osborne, is also the chair of Sun Life Financial, the former CEO of Ontario Power Generation, former CEO of Bell Canada and a director of the Canada Media Fund. David Emerson was the Canadian minister of foreign affairs, Robert Steacy was senior financial officer for Torstar, owner of the *Toronto Star*, director of Domtar Inc., director of Cineplex Galaxy theatres and a director of CIBC.[2]

Postmedia newspapers include: *National Post*; *Calgary Herald*; *Edmonton Journal*; *Financial Post*; *Gazette*, Montreal; *Regina Leader-Post*; *Ottawa Citizen*; *StarPhoenix*, Saskatoon; *Times-Colonist*, Victoria; *Windsor Star*; *Vancouver Sun*; *The Province* (B.C.).

Shaw Communications Inc.

Shaw Communications, based in Calgary, began life in 1966 as a small cable operation but steadily expanded so that by February 2010 it was able to take over CanWest Global's television network. This new entity called Shaw Media shot into the front rank of the Canadian media world. The Global TV network is Canada's third largest. Its national news program has a large following, but it spends relatively little on news-gathering and reporters. Similarly, its entertainment programming has the weakest Canadian content of all the networks. In exchange for taking over the Global network, Shaw had to promise the CRTC that it would spend more on original Canadian entertainment and documentaries. We might hope that they will keep that pledge.

Rogers Communications Inc.

Rogers controls telecommunications, cable TV, high-speed internet distribution services and several magazines. Most people know Rogers as a cable TV provider, but through their ownership of *Macleans* magazine and website they also control a key mouthpiece for right-wing opinion. Rogers sports division includes the Rogers Centre, formerly Toronto's Sky Dome, a financial disaster, bailed out by the citizens of Ontario, then picked up by Rogers for a fraction of its original cost.

Quebecor Inc.

Quebecor, based in Montreal, is one of the largest media companies in Canada and even more diversified than BCE. It grew to its position from a base in paper production, supplying not only newspapers but other paper markets worldwide. In the 1950s its founder Pierre Peladeau (1925–1997) saw the need to push into other business sectors so he began to expand vertically, horizontally and diagonally. As the profits in paper-making have declined, Quebecor has defined itself primarily as a media company. It has succeeded, therefore, in a strategy of convergence where its much larger rivals Seagram and BCE failed. The splashy swagger of its announcement to start a right-wing TV network shows the confidence of Peladeau's son Pierre Karl. For some observers Quebecor symbolizes the new Quebec. It now stands as a powerful Quebec-owned giant moving to global status.

Quebecor illustrates the growth of corporate media and also shows the power in contemporary Quebec, no longer second-fiddle to English business. Quebecor is the parent company of Sun Media newspapers, TVA television production and broadcasting, Vidéotron cable TV distribution, book publishers, magazines and printing companies. With its purchase of Vidéotron, Quebec's largest cable TV operator, Quebecor now owns software and hardware — the product and the means of distribution. It has reached the big leagues, along with BCE and Rogers.

> "I firmly believe that companies that do not have a global vision do not have a future," [Pierre Karl] bellowed at a Quebecor meeting in April as he outlined his dot-com ambitions. The same week, during an evening online chat with devotees of Quebecor's Canoe Web portal, he promised: "We intend to grow — big time — with Quebecor Media." You could almost sense the drive that went into each keystroke.[3]

Power Corporation

If Quebecor represents new money, Power Corp shows the longevity of the old. Although its media holdings, centred in the company Gesca, and its papers, especially *La Presse*, are small compared to BCE and Quebecor, its influence stretches far and wide. Power Corp, in the form of Paul Desmarais its CEO, often seems to work like an invisible hand directing commercial and government policies. When Canadian shipping was big business, Paul Martin, later the prime minister, ran Power's subsidiary Canada Steamship Lines. Like Quebecor it began with staples, water power and electric systems, and now generates the most revenue through insurance.

Corus Entertainment Inc.

Corus is a media and entertainment company with interests in radio and television broadcasting and the production and distribution of children's media content. Corus's principal assets include forty radio stations and a variety of specialty television networks focused on children, such as Treehouse TV and YTV. It also owns Nelvana Limited, home of Babar and Franklin the Turtle, plus Kids Can Press, Canada's largest children's book publisher.

The Irving Empire

The Irving Group of Companies is a family-owned affair of more than three-hundred companies, most based in New Brunswick. They hold a complete monopoly on all daily and weekly newspapers in the province, and as anyone who lives there knows, the Irving name crops up almost everywhere you go, from gas stations to power stations, pulp and paper operations, etc. The family has wielded this power since the 1920s.

Throughout these years, many examples of direct censorship and a strong undertow of political influence have become apparent. Most journalists who work for the Irvings know what is acceptable and what is not. For example, in 2009, a young journalist at the *Telegraph-Journal* was, according to most observers, fired for writing an article that quoted people who had damaged the relationship between the University of New Brunswick and the newspaper.[4] The fact that Irving holds a newspaper monopoly makes it even more problematic when the CBC cuts journalists in the province.

Erin Steuter, who has studied the Irving media for many years, describes the papers as uniformly conservative. "Sometimes, if you track one topic," she says, "you can see slight differences, but they're really very homogenous." The Irving papers are "often very critical of the McCains, who are their direct competitors," says Steuter. "The only deep investigative journalism that you see in the Irving papers is about the McCains." "I think the politicians in power, and those who think they have access to power don't want to mess with the Irvings on any front."[5]

Canadian Radio-Television and Telecommunications Commission — CRTC

The CRTC, established in 1968, is an arm's-length government agency whose mandate is to interpret the Broadcasting Act, of 1991, and the Telecommunications Act, of 1993. It makes rules and sets standards. Most of its work requires public consultation with all interested parties. The Broadcasting and Telecommunications Acts use broad language to set out the government's principles and goals. Thus, the CRTC holds significant power to interpret that language. For this reason, since the late 1990s, various government ministers have tried to exert influence over important decisions. In 2010, it was speculated that Prime Minister Harper had tried to influence the CRTC to allow Sun TV a special licence.

Some of the more important and controversial of its rulings include:

- imposing the 35 percent Canadian music content rule for radio stations;
- assigning licences and renewals for all radio stations;
- creating limits on media company ownership — not more than one newspaper or TV station in any one market or region;
- balancing power between TV networks and cable companies;
- imposing rules for TV and gaming violence;
- regulating the switch to digital TV; and
- deciding whether or not to regulate the internet.

Family Dynasties

Don't Call Him "Junior"

"The loud-talking, Harley-riding, larger-than-life CEO of Calgary's Shaw Communications has just never fit the profile of your typical

Canadian Titan," wrote Thomas Watson, in the March 15, 2010, issue of *Canadian Business.* In November 2010 Shaw was forced to retire early because of his "rudeness."[6]

Canadian newspapers and magazines have often worked hard to create stars of the country's young media tycoons. Ironically, that treatment rarely gets applied to Canadian actors. Many of the people who make up the new generation of media bosses have received kindly biographies. Most highlight their maverick personalities, striving to make their mark in worlds created by their fathers and grandfathers. Jim Shaw, Leonard Asper and Pierre Karl Peladeau in particular seem to stake their reputations on ruffling feathers, making a splash, building a bigger empire. They hope we'll forget the story of young Edgar Bronfman Jr., who in 1994 took over his family liquor and media companies and promptly ran them to the edge of bankruptcy, in the process at one point costing his uncle and father $1 billion a month.[7]

When an earlier generation of newspaper families died out in the 1990s, Peter C. Newman declared that family dynasties were dead.[8] But since then the family business has reasserted itself in the corporate media.

The Son Also Rises

What do the following media heavy-weights have in common? They are all the sons of former media tycoons.

Edward Samuel Rogers is the deputy chair of Rogers Communications Inc., the son of Ted Rogers Jr. (1933–2008), president and CEO of Rogers, and the grandson of Edward Rogers (1900–1939), the founder of the company.

Leonard Asper was until 2010 the president and CEO of CanWest Global Communications. He is the son of Izzy Asper (1932–2003), founder of CanWest Global.

Pierre Karl Peladeau is president and CEO of Quebecor Inc. and son of Pierre Peladeau (1925–1997), founder of the company.

David Thomson is chair of the board of Thomson Reuters. He is the son of Ken Thomson (1923–2006), who at the time of his death was the richest man in Canada, and the grandson of Lord Roy Thomson (1894–1976), who controlled a large media empire, including the *Times* of London.

James K. Irving is co-owner, with his brothers, of the family-owned Irving Group of Companies. He is the son of K.C. Irving (1899–1992) and the grandson of J.D. Irving, the founder of J.D. Irving Ltd.

Paul and André Desmarais are the co-CEOs and presidents of Power Corporation, founded by Paul Desmarais Senior. André is married to former Prime Minister, Jean Chrétien's daughter. Former prime minister, Paul Martin Jr., worked for Paul Senior.

Jim and Brad Shaw are the former and present CEOs of Shaw Communications and the sons of James (J.R.) Shaw, founder of the company and a board member at Suncor Energy.

And One Daughter

Heather A. Shaw is executive chair of the board for Corus Entertainment, Inc. She is the sister of Jim and Brad Shaw, and daughter of J.R. Shaw.

NOTES

Chapter One: The Crisis of Quality

1. *Maclean's*, June 23, 2010.
2. The Alliance for Children and Television et al., *The Case for Kids Programming: Children's and Youth Screen-Based Production in Canada — 2009 Edition* (Banff, June 9, 2009).
3. Said Business School, Unniversity of Oxford, London, September 12, 2008. The most recent Oxford global broadband study can be found at <http://www.sbs.ox.ac.uk/newsandevents/news/Pages/globalbroadbandquality.aspx>. Technology specialist Peter Nowak argues that the study showed that "Canada had squandered its lead as an early broadband leader." See "Canada's broadband networks not ready for future," *Globe and Mail*, September 15, 2008, and Berkman Center for Internet and Society, Harvard University, *Next Generation Connectivity: A Review of Broadband Internet Transitions and Policy from around the World* <http://www.fcc.gov/stage/pdf/Berkman_Center_Broadband_Study_13Oct09.pdf>.
4. The entire Senate report is available free online, "Final Report on the Canadian News Media," Vol. 1 of 2, June 2006 <www.parl.gc.ca>.
5. Quoted in Trudie Richards, "Public Relations and the Westray Mine Explosion," in *The Westray Chronicles: A Case Study in Corporate Crime* (Halifax: Fernwood, 1999).
6. Richard Siklos, *Shades of Black: Conrad Black: His Rise and Fall* (Toronto: McClelland and Stewart, 2004).
7. "National Radio News Reporter Survey, April 2010." Leaked report

published by Friends of Canadian Broadcasting, May 8, 2010.

8.　David McKie, "The Canadian Military Should Break with History and Stop Keeping Secrets," *Freedom to Read, 2010* (Toronto: Book and Periodical Council of Canada, 2010).

9.　Bill Curry, "Access to Information Risks Being 'Obliterated': Report," *Globe and Mail*, April 13, 2010.

1-.　Mike De Souza, "Climate Change Scientists Feel Muzzled," *Montreal Gazette*, March 15, 2010.

11.　Mary Vipond, *The Mass Media in Canada, Third Edition* (Toronto: Lorimer, 2000), p. 5.

Chapter Two: Forms, Styles and Genres

1.　Jim Leach, *Film in Canada* (Toronto: Oxford, 2006), p. 66.

2.　Leach, *Film in Canada*, p. 77.

3.　Nat Shuster, "*Wuthering Heights* on the St. Lawrence," *Motion*, Nov./Dec. 1973, quoted in Leach, *Film in Canada*, p. 80.

4.　Leach, *Film in Canada*, p. 19.

5.　John Doyle, "What makes Canadian TV so different," in *Television Quarterly*, July 27, 2007.

6.　Alex Beam, "Copping out on Canada," *Boston Globe*, July 21, 2010.

7.　Jason Silverman, "Loretta Todd," *The Canadian Encyclopedia* <www.canadianencyclopedia.ca>.

8.　Kathleen Lippa, "Super Shamou flies again," Northern News Services, Baker Lake, February 7, 2005.

9.　Not all these essay programs are as conventional, however, as shown by David Suzuki's popular and long-running *The Nature of Things* (1960–) ; with Suzuki after 1979).

10.　Darrell Varga, "The Image of the 'People' in CBC's *Canada: A People's History*," in Malek Khouri and Varga, eds. *Working On Screen: Representations of the Working Class in Canadian Cinema* (Toronto: University of Toronto Press, 2006), p. 75.

11.　See in particular, David Frank, "In Search of the Canadian Labour Film," in Khouri, *Working on Screen*, p. 40–41.

12.　Rick Salutin, "The cleanest history ever told," *Globe and Mail*, January 19, 2001. See also David Frank, "Public History and the People's History: A View from Atlantic Canada," *Acadiensis* 32, 2 (Spring 2003), pp. 120–33. Also valuable are the collected responses to the series at <http://www.carleton.ca/ccph/historycollaborative/>.

13. David Hogarth, *Documentary Television in Canada* (Toronto: University of Toronto Press, 2002), p. 46.

14. Cinema Direct is the term used in Quebec to describe the documentary movement begun in the late 1950s that emphasized observation over narration, the speech of ordinary Québécois, the community links between filmmakers and their subjects, and the use of new lighter-weight cameras and sound recorders. Although based on observation, in Cinema Direct, filmmakers did not want to position themselves as distant from the people in their films, which was more the case in American Direct Cinema, French cinéma vérité and English-Canada's candid eye films.

15. Michel Euvard and Pierre Véronneau, "Direct Cinema," in Véronneau and Piers Handling, eds., *Self Portrait* (Ottawa: Canadian Film Institute, 1980).

16. See Tom Waugh et al., eds., *Challenge for Change: Activist Documentary at the National Film Board of Canada* (Montreal: McGill-Queen's University Press, 2010).

17. Paul Rutherford, *When Television Was Young* (Toronto: University of Toronto Press, 1990), pp. 382–83.

18. For a fascinating look at the making of this controversial film and much about India, see Devyani Saltzman's *Shooting Water* (Toronto: Key Porter, 2005).

19. "ACTRA performers call on CRTC to put more Canada in Prime Time," CRTC Hearing, November 25, 2009.

20. CRTC hearing.

21. "Canada: Bullish Billions," *Time Magazine* April 30, 1951.

22. Hilda Neatby, quoted in Rutherford, *When Television Was Young*, p. 14.

23. Keith Hampson, Museum of Broadcast Communications, Chicago <www.museumtv.com>.

24. John Doyle, "Beating up the CBC is like beating up a sick puppy," *Globe and Mail*, April 28, 2010.

25. Suite 101: Talk radio fires up the airways: Radio's most controversial personalities have some radical opinions <http://canadianhistory.suite101>.

26. Canadian Newspaper Association <http://www.cna-acj.ca/en/daily-newspaper-paid-circulation-data>.

27. Statistics on circulation and advertising revenues can be found in *The State of the Newsmedia* annual reports, published by the Pew Research Centre at <www.journalism.org> and also at the *World Association of Newspapers Annual Reports* <www.wan-ifra.org>.

28. Peter C. Newman, *Titans: How the New Canadian Establishment Seized Power* (Toronto: Penguin, 1999), p. 268.

29. Richard Siklos, "A mind-boggling deal…" *Globe and Mail*, December 12, 2008. At the time of writing The *Los Angeles Times* is still operating under bankruptcy protection.

30. I am not alone in this opinion. I take my cues from many experienced media analysts, such as Peter Preston and Roy Greenslade, of the *Guardian* in Britain, Juan Antonio Giner of the Spanish newspaper design group, Innovation, and Eric Pfanner of the *New York Times*. David Estok, late of *The Hamilton Spectator*, says essentially the same thing. See David Estok, "Reports of newspapers' death greatly exaggerated." *J-Source*, April 20, 2010. See also David Olive, "Newspapers now bouncing back," *Toronto Star*, February 13, 2011.

31. *The Canadian Press Stylebook*, XI edition (Toronto: The Canadian Press, 1999), p. 325.

32. Robb Montgomery, Presentation, 12th World Editors Forum, Seoul, Korea, May 31, 2005.

33. School of Journalism and Mass Communications, San José State University. "Grade the News" <www.gradethenews.org>.

34. See the School of Journalism, Kansas University <www.web.ku.edu>.

Chapter Three: The Big Issues

1. Marsha Barber and Ann Rauhala, "The Canadian News Directors Study: Demographics and Political Leanings of Television Decision Makers," *Canadian Journal of Communication*, 30, 2 (2005).

2. Frances Henry and Carol Tator, *Deconstructing the "Rightness of Whiteness" in Television Commercials, News and Programming* (research report submitted to the Prairie Centre of Excellence for Research on Immigration and Integration, February 2003).

3. Rita Shelton Deverell, "Who Will Inherit the Airwaves," *Canadian Journal of Communications*, 34, 1 (2009).

4. Vipond, *The Mass Media in Canada*, p. 2.

5. Mark Raboy, *Missed Opportunities: The Story of Canada's Broadcasting Policy* (Toronto: University of Toronto Press, 1990), p. 338.

6. This represents less than 30 percent of Hollywood's income, with the rest coming from video and TV sales and a growing amount from the international box office. See Bill Briggs, "Hollywood sees year of 'Paranormal Activity'," MSNBC, February 2, 2010, and Toby Miller et al., *Global Hollywood*

2 (London: BFI Publishing, 2008).

7. Christopher McCormick, *The Westray Chronicles: A Case Study in Corporate Crime* (Halifax: Fernwood Publishing, 1999), p. 190.

8. See Robert Babe, "Newspaper Discourses on Environment," in Jeffrey Klaehn, ed., *Filtering the News: Essays on Herman and Chomsky's Propaganda Model* (Montreal: Black Rose Books, 2005), quoted in James Winter, *Lies the Media Tell Us* (Montreal: Black Rose Books, 2007).

9. Winter, *Lies the Media Tell Us,* pp. 48–49.

10. See Paul Rutherford, *Endless Propaganda: The Advertising of Public Goods* (Toronto: University of Toronto Press, 2000).

11. The Royal Commission on Newspapers, 1981 (Kent Commission) can be found at Canadian Govt. Pub. Centre Supply and Services Canada. ISBN 9780660109541. For a short overview, see "Newspaper Ownership in Canada: An Overview of the Davey and Kent Commission Studies," by Joseph Jackson, Political and Social Affairs Division, Government of Canada, December 17, 1999.

12. Tom Kent, "Concentration with Convergence — Goodbye, Freedom of the Press," *Policy Options,* October 2002, p. 27.

13. Erin Steuter, "Freedom of the Press Is for Those Who Own One: The Irving Media Monopoly in New Brunswick," *The Dominion,* October 11, 2003.

14. Susan Krashinsky, "SunTV to launch without CRTC help," *Globe and Mail,* June 14, 2010.

15. Raboy, *Missed Opportunities,* pp. xii–xiii.

16. Henry Srebrnik, "Who rules the airwaves in Canada?" *Guardian,* August 27, 2004.

17. Jay Bryan, "CRTC should not be censor," *Montreal Gazette,* July 15, 2004.

18. Garry Toffoli, Associate Editor, <www.monarchist.ca> October 1998.

19. For a broad survey and analysis of the new right in Canada, see Marci McDonald, *The Armageddon Factor* (Toronto: Random House, 2010). The *Calgary Star*'s reviewer called the book "shrill nonsense."

Chapter Four: Media in Quebec

1. Claude Bélanger, Professor of History, Marianopolis College, Montreal, <http://faculty.marianopolis.edu/c.belanger/quebechistory/about.htm>.

2. Lise Payette, "Les deux peuples fondateurs" ["The Two Founding Peoples"], *Le Devoir,* April 9, 2010.

3. Primarily SODEC, Société de développement des entreprises culturelles.

4. See Guy Fournier, *What About Tomorrow?* (Ottawa: CRTC and Telefilm Canada, May 2003).

5. Myriam Fontaine, *Canadian Encyclopedia* <http://www.thecanadianency-clopedia.com>.

6. See Richard Poplak, "Two Cultures, One Cheque — The Real Hollywood North," *This Magazine*, November 2005, and Denis Seguin, "Success to Excess: Made-in-Quebec Movies," *Canadian Business Online*, September 11, 2006.

7. Manon Lamontagne, Museum of Broadcast Communications <www.museumtv>.

8. Patricia Bailey, "Julie Snyder: TV host dynamo and blockbuster producer," *Playback*, August 20, 2007.

9. "A new generation of Quebec filmmakers captures a culture adrift," *This Magazine*, July 6, 2010.

10. See André Loiselle, "*Look* like a worker and *Act* like a worker: Stereotypical Representations of the Working Class in Quebec Fiction films," in Khouri, *Working On Screen*, pp. 207–34.

11. See Bill Marshall, *Quebec National Cinema* (Kingston: McGill-Queen's University Press, 2001) for a theoretical discussion of these issues.

12. Michel Euvard and Pierre Véronneau, "Direct Cinema."

13. For a detailed critique of the film in its historical context and the crucial role of Michel Brault, see André Loiselle, *Cinema as History: Michel Brault and Modern Quebec* (Toronto: Toronto International Film Festival Group, 2007).

14. André Loiselle, in *Cinema as History*, describes the critical reception to the film, some of which was negative because the film didn't provide a straight documentary treatment of the events.

15. See <http://www.altercine.org/html/en/temoignages.php>.

16. Matthew Hays, "Immigrant Song," *Montreal Mirror*, April 24, 2008.

17. Linda Leith, "Quebec should rethink its relationship with anglophones," *Gazette*, September 27, 2010.

18. Chantal Hébert, "Quebec media have power to stir niqab debate," *Toronto Star*, April 5, 2010.

19. See Fournier, *What About Tomorrow.*

Chapter Five: The New Media

1. Like most definitions involving culture and communications, the concept of new media exhibits "fuzzy boundaries" and an ever-changing landscape.

2. See Don Tapscott's description of his book *Grown Up Digital: How the Net Generation Is Changing the World* at his website <http://dontapscott.com>.

3. For this point in particular, see Tucker Harding, "Digital Natives and Digital Immigrants," Columbia Center for New Media Teaching and Learning, December 14, 2010 <http://ccnmtl.columbia.edu/enhanced/primers/digital_natives.html>.

4. See Brian Winston, *Media, Technology and Society: A History: From the Telegraph to the Internet* (London: Routledge, 1998).

5. See Dan Schiller, *Digital Capitalism: Networking the Global Market System* (Boston: MIT Press, 2000), p. 209.

6. Unnamed blogger quoted by Hamersley, "Time to blog on," *Guardian*, May 20, 2002, p. 38.

7. October 9, 2007.

8. Some of these folks would make Marshall McLuhan blush — Canada's Don Tapscott, for example, who can write sensible political and economic analysis when he wants to.

9. "Paul Sullivan's view of citizen journalism," transcript of an interview with Ira Basen for CBC Radio, June 17, 2009.

10. See *PressThink*, June 17, 2006.

11. Stephen Hui, "First Nations seeking to cross digital divide," *straight.com*, July 16, 2009.

12. Iain Marlow and Jacquie McNish, "Canada's digital divide," *Globe and Mail*, April 3, 2010.

13. The Canadian Internet Project lists as its sponsors many of the dominant media corporations in the country plus the federal government, the Interactive Advertising Bureau of Canada, and ebay.ca.

14. Marlow and McNish, "Canada's digital divide." See also Ipsos Reid, "Older Canadians and the Internet," February 15, 2007 <http://ipsosna.com>.

Chapter Six: Investigative Reporting

1. David Spark, *Investigative Reporting: A Study in Technique* (Oxford: Focal Press, 1999).

2. Cecil Rosner, *Behind the Headlines: A History of Investigative Reporting in Canada* (Toronto: Oxford University Press, 2008), pp. vi–vii.

3. Maxine Ruvinsky, *Investigative Reporting in Canada* (Toronto: Oxford University Press, 2007), p. xxvii.

4. Ruvinsky, *Investigative Reporting in Canada,* p. xx.

5. McKie in Ruvinsky, *Investigative Reporting in Canada,* p. 345.

6.   Bolan in Ruvinsky, *Investigative Reporting in Canada*, p. xx.
7.   Ruvinsky, "Interview with David Pugliese," in Ruvinsky, *Investigative Reporting in Canada*, p. 97.
8.   "Dying for a job," CBC Radio, April 2006.
9.   "Interview with David McKie," in Ruvinsky, *Investigative Reporting in Canada*, p. 341.
10.   Ruvinsky, *Investigative Reporting in Canada*, p. 352.
11.   "Interview with Lindsay Kines" in Ruvinsky, *Investigative Reporting in Canada*.
12.   See Andrew Mitrovica's detailed analysis of this in "Hear no Evil, Write no Lies," *The Walrus*, December–January, 2007.
13.   See Kim Bolan, *Loss of Faith: How the Air India Bombers Got Away with Murder* (Toronto: McClelland and Stewart, 2005).
14.   See, for instance, "When depression turns ugly," *Globe and Mail*, April 23, 1002.
15.   Ruvinsky, *Investigative Reporting in Canada*, pp. 146–62.
16.   Louise Elliot, "2005 Award Winners," Canadian Association of Journalists website <www.caj.ca/mediamag/awards2006>.
17.   MacDonald in Rosner, *Behind the Headlines*, p. 218.
18.   Tim Naumetz, "Teneycke 'licks wounds' after exit from Sun TV," *The Hill Times online*, September 20, 2010.
19.   Pierre Karl Peladeau, "All's not fair in war," Canoe network, April 27, 2011.

Chapter Seven: Media and Canadian Society

1.   See Roy MacSkimming, *The Perilous Trade: Publishing Canada's Writers* (Toronto: McClelland and Stewart, 2003).
2.   Neilia Sherman, "Top-notch TV Canadian Children's Television," in *iparenting*, <http://www.iparentingcanada.com>.
3.   Noam Chomsky and Edward Herman, *Manufacturing Consent: The Political Economy of the Mass Media* (New York: Pantheon Books, 1988).
4.   Jean Swanson, *Poor Bashing* (Toronto: Between the Lines, 2001).
5.   Jonathan Freedman, *Media Violence and Its Effect on Aggression: Assessing the Scientific Evidence* (Toronto: University of Toronto Press, 2002).
6.   Cynthia Carter and Kay Weaver, *Violence and the Media* (London: Open University, 2003).
7.   See Jean Saint-Vil, "What Is Canada Doing in Haiti? The "Ottawa Initiative on Haiti": Humanist Peacekeeping or…?," *Global Research*, April 20, 2009.

8. Thomas M. Griffen, *Haiti: Human Rights Investigation, November 11–21, 2004* (Miami: Centre for the Study of Human Rights, University of Miami School of Law) <http://www.law.miami.edu/cshr/CSHR_Report_02082005_v2.pdf>.

9. Kim Ives, Editorial, *Haiti Liberté,* 3 52, July 14, 2010.

10. John Doyle, "The obsession with the military," *Globe and Mail*, December 14, 2006.

11. Peter Mansbridge, "Letter to the Editor," *Globe and Mail*, December 15, 2006.

12. See Michael Geist, "Details of transition to digital TV a little blurry," *Toronto Star,* February 16, 2009. This and many other important recommendations were made by the Canadian Media Guild in its submission to the CRTC Public Hearings, July 18, 2007, entitled "The most diversity for the most Canadians."

13. Richard Keshen and Kent MacAskill, "I Told You So: Newspaper Ownership in Canada and the Kent Commission Twenty Years Later," *American Review of Canadian Studies*, 30, 3, Autumn, 2000.

Appendix

1. Khouri, *Working on Screen,* p. 84.

2. "Postmedia Network… Directors Announced." *Financial Post* media release, July 19, 2010.

3. Konrad Yakabuski, "The conversion of Pierre Karl Péladean," *Globe and Mail*, May 26, 2000.

4. See Regan Ray "Intern fired over news article," *J-source*, June 8, 2009 <http://www.j-source.ca/english_new/detail.php?id=3926?>.

5. Dru Oja Jay, *Misnomer* blog, "Interview with Dr. Erin Stouter, August 12, 2002." See also the NB Media Co-op <www.nbmediacoop.org>.

6. "Shaw denies rudeness sank CEO early," CBC News, November 19, 2010.

7. See Brian Milner, "The Unmasking of a Dynasty," *Cigar Aficionado*, April 1, 2003.

8. Peter C. Newman, *Titans*, pp. 21–77.

ACKNOWLEDGEMENTS

Thanks first off to Errol Sharpe of Fernwood for his invitation to write this book and to join the fine writers in the "About Canada" series. Thanks also to the following for their invaluable comments on the manuscript: Blaine Allan, of Queen's University; Josh Bloch of the CBC; Michele Lemon, of Sheridan College; Ryan Young, of John Abbot College; Jane Springer, writer and editor; Matt Adams of rabble.ca; and Riali Johannesson, lawyer and activist. I'd also like to thank those folks who provided support and comments, including Richard Swift, Sally Miller, Barbara Emanuel, Marilyn Legge, Imbi Kannel, Renée Knapp, Chuck Kleinhans, Marc Glassman, Peter Saunders, Has Malik, Mary Sue Rankin, Annie McClelland, and of course, as always, my partner Geri Sadoway.

Lastly, I am very grateful to all the Fernwood Publishing and Brunswick Books people: my editor, Brenda Conroy, Beverley Rach, Wayne Antony, Nancy Malek, and the incomparable duo, Lindsay Sharpe and Michael Jackel.